THE PHYSICAL SIDE
OF THINKING

THE PHYSICAL SIDE
OF THINKING

By

LEELA C. ZION, Ph.D.

Humboldt State University
Arcata, California

BETTY LOU RAKER, Ed.D.

California State University, Chico
Chico, California

CHARLES C THOMAS • PUBLISHER
Springfield • Illinois • U.S.A.

Published and Distributed Throughout the World by
CHARLES C THOMAS • PUBLISHER
2600 South First Street
Springfield, Illinois 62717

© *1986 by* CHARLES C THOMAS • PUBLISHER
ISBN 0-398-05171-2
Library of Congress Catalog Card Number: 85-14827

With THOMAS BOOKS *careful attention is given to all details of manufacturing
and design. It is the Publisher's desire to present books that are satisfactory as to their
physical qualities and artistic possibilities and appropriate for their particular use.*
THOMAS BOOKS *will be true to those laws of quality that assure a good name
and good will.*

Printed in the United States of America
Q-R-3

Library of Congress Cataloging in Publication Data
Zion, Leela C.
  The physical side of thinking.

  Bibliography: p.
  Includes index.
  1. Perceptual-motor learning. 2. Movement education.
I. Raker, Betty Lou. II. Title.
LB1067.Z56   1985   370.15'23   85-14827
ISBN 0-398-05171-2

PREFACE

I N *The Physical Side of Thinking* we have woven together a fabric of concepts and activities designed to shed light on the emerging subject of "perceptualmotor development." A good many learning handicaps are the result of inadequate development of perceptualmotor skills, and it is our contention that a practical understanding of the factors that contribute to perceptualmotor development will aid teachers as they work with children.

At the heart of this discussion we introduce the *ZISC,* a perceptualmotor diagnostic and remediation tool. Based on the ideas of Newell Kephart, Bryant Cratty and Ray Barsch, the ZISC is designed for use in the classroom. It is individualized yet it can be administered quickly. It is keyed in such a way that specific perceptualmotor weaknesses can be identified quickly. The ZISC is followed by a lengthy collection of developmental activities suitable for use with preschool and elementary school children.

Each child, on entering the educational setting, is assumed to have reached the psycho-physiological maturation of a five- or six-year-old. It is upon this base of *assumed perceptualmotor capabilities* that the teacher begins to build cognitive skills. Teachers in succeeding classrooms continue in this vein. Over time some students develop labels — *Troublemaker, Slow Learner, Poor Listener, Underachiever, Shy.* The fact is, many students don't perform well in reading, math, and higher-level abstract thinking, and we have found that where cognitive skills are poorly developed, often perceptualmotor skills are also poorly developed. Hence our interest in the ZISC.

The ZISC provides a relatively quick and easy way to reduce the number of students with learning handicaps because it provides teachers with a straightforward method by which to identify and develop skill in eleven different perceptualmotor diagnostic integration areas. The

ZISC will be particularly useful to preschool teachers, teachers of handicapped students, physical education teachers, and recreation therapists.

Our analysis includes discussions of subjects that have traditionally been considered disparate: the sensory system; neuroanatomy and neurophysiology; physical development; balance, rhythm, and coordination; movement mastery; split-brain research; time and space interrelationships; body concept. Like Clara Lee Edgar, Kenneth A. Leithwood, and Newell C. Kephart, we find significant and important relationships among these subjects. Our ideas follow the work of Jean Piaget.

ACKNOWLEDGMENTS

MANY PEOPLE have contributed to the development of the ideas that led to the writing of this book.

We owe a large debt of gratitude to those who have been our teachers through the years: T. Bentley Edwards, Newell Kephart, Ray Barsch, Bryant Cratty, Jane W. Shurmer, Lew D. Oliver, Vesta Holt, and Valerie Hunt.

We are indebted to those who have been our students through the years: Abby Abinanti, Penny Benson Brush, Roger Harvey, Barbara Briezy, Mary Hill, Wanda Hansen, Cindy Nelson, Sharon Galligan, Judy O'Neill, Fran Coslet, Penny and Jim Sweet, and Lynn Warner.

We are grateful to our colleagues: Don Mahler, Toni Martin, James D. Belluzzi, Shirley Smith, and Jim Huff.

We have much gratitude for the very precise and helpful work of our editor, Jody Lawlor.

Our most eternal and infinite gratitude and love goes to our mothers, Grace Sifford Raker and Clarice Davis Zion.

In order to avoid sexism, we have alternated the pronouns he and she throughout the text.

CONTENTS

LIST OF FIGURES

THE PHYSICAL SIDE
OF THINKING

CHAPTER I

INTRODUCTION

PURPOSE

OUR INTENT herein is to weave a fabric that will join the conceptual basis of perceptualmotor development with a developmental sequence of ideas and activities. The ideas and activities are designed to help the reader think while he is moving and think even when he is through moving. Each chapter is concerned with the development of those concepts that join the strands of PMD (perceptualmotor development) with activities that the reader can do on his own to help grasp the verbal and nonverbal ideas being demonstrated. These are *adult* PMD experiences designed to lend concrete experience to a theoretical construct. Youngsters may be able to use some of these activities if the activities are adjusted for age, skill, and purpose. There are many excellent books on PMD activities for children listed in the bibliography.

SENSING, MOVING, AND THINKING

We hope to demonstrate the interrelationship of sensing, moving, and thinking, an interrelationship that is essential in all living creatures whether at a conscious level or not. This interrelationship develops out of the individual's interaction with the environment (Piaget, 1954) and can therefore be either haphazardly or efficiently developed.

When the sensing-moving-thinking interrelationship develops magically and haphazardly out of an infant's months of interaction with an environment, people tend to think:

1. *Experience is the teacher.*
2. *Learning is explained by:*

> *Chance as the designer of experience*
> *Trial and error*
> *Maturation of biological givens*
> *Repetitions to perfect habituated motor skills.*

3. *There is (or is not) a congenital capacity to profit from experience in terms of cognitive, psychomotor, and affective learning.*

A perceptualmotor program is built on a different set of ideas:

1. *The infant constructs a world that is learned.*
2. *Construction of comprehension is the result of:*
   Intent as the designer of experiences
   Multiple success attempts
   Development of functional processes
   Variations to generalize flexible motor patterns.
3. *There is a congenital capacity to structure experience in terms of increasingly more profound and complex relationships.*

Mental processing is the result of a functioning body. What we do and do not do to our bodies is vitally important to every facet of our lives. There is an interrelationship of process that is dynamic, ongoing, ever-changing. Piaget made great strides in analyzing the developmental sequences of intellectual growth. He divided these into periods: first, the *sensorimotor period;* second, the *preoperational period;* third, the *concrete operational period;* and fourth, the *formal operational period.* Throughout the learning process Piaget stressed the point that you cannot teach concepts verbally, that they must be taught through activity (Piaget, 1972).

Moving, awareness, thinking, and learning are all processes that are interrelated and contribute to each other. Sometimes our culture or physiology causes us to separate these processes from each other which can create a physical or mental "deficit." The work of Charles Tart of the University of California at Davis provides an illustration.

Tart (1963) performed an experiment which involved seating a subject in a soundproof room, wired to record brain waves, heart rate, galvanic skin response, muscular activity, and respiratory changes. In another room in the same building, a second person was electrically shocked at random intervals. The first subject was asked to decide when the second person was being shocked. The results were that there was no relation between the subject's *conscious* guesses when the shocks occurred and the actual events. *But,* the subject's *physiological changes* at the instances when the second subject was being shocked were statistically significant. On a fundamental perceptualmotor level the first subject *knew* what was happening, but on a conscious level she had no immediate access to this information.

How often do these processes fail to interrelate in the academic world? the athletic world? the loving world?

CHILD AS PHYSICIST AND KINESIOLOGIST

By the time a normal youngster is two, she is a physicist extraordinaire (Barsch, 1968) and has internal constructs that guide movements relating to such things as: (1) gravity, (2) static and dynamic equilibrium, (3) motion, (4) leverage, (5) force, (6) space/time, (7) mass/weight, and (8) inertia energy.

The two-year old is also a kinesiologist, knowing which muscles to contract and to what degree while other muscles are relaxed for every slight or large movement of the body. As her interactions with the environment continue to increase, so do the refinements in all these knowledges (practices). The individual becomes an accomplished "terrenaut," comparable to an accomplished cosmonaut, in her ability to use these constructs.

KEPHART

Much of the work of Newell Kephart (1971) undergirds our approach to PMD because we believe that his theoretical treatment of perceptualmotor development is the most logical. We hope to demonstrate this throughout the book. There is probably more research substantiating Kephart's concepts than any other investigator in the field (Edgar, 1967; Leithwood, 1971).

PHYSICAL MEASURES CORRELATED WITH MENTAL MEASURES

Many in education, especially in physical education, have believed that there *must* be some relationship between the functioning body and the functioning mind. In the late nineteenth century, anthropometrists measured height and weight and correlated those measures with varying measures of intelligence, grades, and test scores. They did not find significant correlations. In the 1930s Gates measured physical abilities like agility, strength, and speed to see if they correlated positively with I.Q., but they did not. The results were positive but not significant.

It has only been in the past two decades that researchers have found significant correlations among complex movement abilities like dynamic balance (Warner, 1970) or gymnastic movement patterns (Leithwood, 1971) and reading, I.Q., grades, or teacher evaluations.

Smith and Smith (1962), working with delayed visual feedback in order to understand specific human motion patterns, determined that the distinguishing characteristics of behavior are defined by the basic mechanisms of perceptualmotor integration. They believe that motion and perception are inseparably related. Edgar (1967, 1970, 1975) studied handicapped youngsters following the guidelines of Piaget and Kephart (1971) and found that sensorimotor training programs significantly improved performance on Adaptive, Language, and Personal-Social scales. Edgar theorizes that there is a general intellectual gain with increased sensorimotor integration.

PSYCHOMOTOR AND PERCEPUTALMOTOR

To the uninitiated, movement programs probably "all look alike." There are vast differences, however, when one begins to employ them. Gallahue (1976) defines psychomotor development as "learning to move with control and efficiency through space." The term *motor development* is often used interchangeably with *psychomotor development,* indicating a tendency to separate the motor mechanisms from the sensory systems and environmental stimuli.

PMD programs are: (1) efforts to change the basic knowledge-gathering and environment-structuring strategies and capacities of the child, (2) designed to make poor movers become efficient movers, thereby making poor information-creators become good information-creators and making poor readers and mathematicians become better readers and mathematicians, and (3) efforts to change perceptual function through activities in order to change perceptualmotor structure, in order to change future perceptualmotor functioning.

Psychomotor activities are often essential to perceptualmotor activities since they are often automated movements that have no relation to external stimuli and need no conscious attention. Psychomotor activities may be helpful in a game like basketball which can be perceptualmotor in nature. For instance, an automated dribbling pattern would allow the player the opportunity to look at and think about the location and movements of his teammates and opponents and enable him to make the best possible of plays.

To use an Olympic example, if one were training to put the shot, one would probably be involved in a psychomotor program that would improve motor control and efficiency in a situation where less sensory feedback is necessary for improvement. If one were training for the Olympic basketball team, one would be more successful in a perceptualmotor development program that takes into account environmental changes, such as the movement of opponents and teammates and the necessity for perceptual and motor coordinations to know where to move, when and how and why, and which changes to make from one interrelationship to another.

Further, psychomotor programs are geared more to sports usually labeled *closed,* while perceptualmotor development programs are geared more toward sports usually labeled *open*. A closed sport is one in which the activity of the performer is separated from the activity of the opponent in space/time, resulting in activity with little, if any, essential feedback needed about the opponent. In putting the shot one really only needs to know where the circle is and where the markers are before starting an automatic set of movement patterns that have been prelearned. Sports of a similar nature are other field events, gymnastics, bowling, archery, and golf. The main sensory information necessary is the proprioception or kinesthesia of the movement itself. In open sports, in addition to closed skills, one also needs information about the movements of opponents and teammates; one's own location in relation to them and the goal; the particular qualities of each player and oneself so that proprioception of the movements can be much more flexible and adaptable to the particular instance in space/time. Sports of this nature include basketball, soccer, field hockey, football, tennis, badminton, and racquetball.

Perceptualmotor development deals with all incoming information, its integration with pertinent previous experiences, and the selection of appropriate responses. Most athletes are highly trained in psychomotor skills rather than perceptualmotor skills even though a PMD program would be an advantage.

If I were to give you a large rubber playground ball and ask you to describe how you would use it in a psychomotor way, what would you say? There are several correct answers, of course. You might say, "Practice over and over hitting a target as accurately or with as much speed as possible." If I were to ask you how you would use that same ball in a perceputalmotor way, what would you say? You might say, "Throw it against the wall in as many different ways as possible," or "Bounce the ball under each leg as you walk across the room." These examples are intended to give you an idea about how PMD differs from psychomotor development programs.

Many PMD programs have been lacking in basic assumptions of sound educational development. The result has been confusion for those seeking a comprehensive view of the role of PMD programs in intellectual development or curriculum planning. This book has been developed for those who are investigating PMD programs (elementary school educators, physical educators, preschool educators, recreation specialists, and special educators) for special populations and also for those who wish to improve internal consistency in existing programs.

ACTIVITIES

1. Juggling

A. Use two balls (tennis, handball, racquetball, bean bag, etc.) and teach yourself to juggle. Start with two balls in one hand unless you already know how (in which case try the nondominant hand or three balls in one hand, etc., just so that it challenges you).
B. Practice learning to juggle ten minutes a day for ten days.
C. Keep a log of how well you do by counting catches: 1, 3, 2, 0, 0, 1, 0, 2, 3, etc., *OR* count all catches made in the last thirty seconds of each session, *OR* count the one string of catches that was the longest in a row.
D. By keeping notes, keep track of how you teach yourself and how well you perform.
E. Each day try to analyze your teaching and see what changes or improvements you will make in the next lesson.
F. When all ten lessons are over, analyze your method of teaching in terms of:

psychomotor vs. perceptualmotor
kinesthetic vs. visual
left brain vs. right brain
_____ vs. _____
_____ vs. _____.

G. What did you learn about yourself during this experiment? As learner? As teacher?

2. Two-by-fours

A. With a partner, a blindfold (a dish towel will work fine), an eight-foot 2 x 4 (if possible), and a basketball, start out walking the 2 x 4 with your eyes open and no blindfold. Walk forward, then backward, then slide sideways (no crossover). Then have your partner do the same.

B. Now put on the blindfold and with your partner holding you under your upper arm or by the hand, again walk forward, backwards, and sideways. Then have your partner do the same.

C. Now with blindfold on, and no contact with your partner (though he will be right with you all the time and will use auditory cues), walk forward, backward, sideways. Have your partner do the same.

D. Now with blindfold on, your partner will bounce the basketball to you at about chest height. You catch it and bounce it back. Do this about ten times and then switch with your partner.

E. Still with the blindfold and basketball, dribble in place while your partner retrieves the ball for you. When you feel more confident, dribble while moving forward. Switch with your partner.

F. *Now* put all of this together. The first time, without blindfold, walk forward down the 2 x 4 while dribbling the basketball. Then do it with the blindfold. Then let your partner try.

G. Since this has been an exercise in something quite unusual (for most), can you figure out what about yourself you changed to be at least somewhat successful in all the above tasks? Can you determine any one strategy that you used throughout these activities?

H. Most people who try this exercise, perform better than they thought they would, especially on the last task; did you? Can you explain your performance?

3. Slap Jack and Animal

Slap Jack and *Animal* spell some of the difference between psychomotor and perceptualmotor.

A. **Slap Jack.** First get a friend and a deck of playing cards. Deal out the deck until each player has half a deck. Cards should be stacked face down. In unison, players draw the top card off their stacks placing the cards face up on the table space between them. When a jack is turned up, both players try to slap the jack before the other. The player slapping the jack first gets the jack plus any other cards that may have accumulated beneath it. The object of the game is to end up with the most cards.

Slap Jack may be varied by increasing or decreasing the possible number of cards that can be slapped. You could elect to just slap one-eyed jacks (there are only two) or you might choose to slap all red cards (there are twenty-six).

The game involves close attention to how many slappable cards have previously been played so as to know the possibility and preparedness for each turning of the cards. It also requires a fast visual assessment of the cards; comparison of cards; and fast reaction time. Slap Jack is primarily a psychomotor game.

B. **Animal.** You really need 4-8 players for this game. Start out by having all players pick animal names for themselves and then proceed to introduce each player by her new name.

Deal the cards out so that all have equal numbers of cards. These should be stacked face down, and as in Slap Jack, they should be drawn off the top and placed right side up in a visible pile close to each player's face-down pile. In this game, players need to look for matchings among the other players. If you and another player turn over the same card at the same time, the player who names the other player's animal name first wins that card and any others that may be under it. Again, the goal is to win the most cards. Now, however, players must scan the whole playing environment to find whether there is a matching card, and players must also recall the new name of the player and say it before the opposition. It is the scanning of the environment and the matching challenges that make Animal a more perceptualmotor game than Slap Jack.

CHAPTER II

THE SENSORY SYSTEM

INTRODUCTION

AS WITH MOST things, PMD becomes clearer when you understand its constituent elements. We will start with the sensory system, a difficult but enlightening facet of PMD.

CENTRAL NERVOUS SYSTEM (CNS)

The central nervous system (CNS) is all of the body's mechanisms for receiving, integrating, sorting, and making decisions about information and acting (or not acting) on those decisions. Our sensory systems are out vehicles for receiving information from our environment and from ourselves. There are more sensory systems than the five typically referred to in many psychology texts (smell, taste, touch, hearing, and sight). *Kinesthesis* (involving four kinds of receptors) and *proprioception* (five kinds of receptors) are two of the lesser known sensory systems: both are associated with sensing movement. It is the information from sensory receptors that determines what we can know. They serve as an interface between our thinking and our environment, and in this way they limit what we can know. There is much information "out there" for which we have no singluar receiving apparatus.

NEURON

Neurons are hypothesized to be the basic building blocks of the CNS. It is the activity of neurons that determines much of our behaivor, and each person has between 20 and 200 billion of them. The specialization of neurons compared with other cells is to communicate with other neurons. The receptive end of a neuron, called a dendrite, receives information. The transmitting end of a neuron, called an axon, releases transmitter fluid into the space between its own axon and the dendrite of one of its neighboring neurons. When the neuron receives a stimulus from another neuron at the dendrite, the axonal membrane undergoes a shift in polarity. When the stimulus is sufficient, the axon opens gates in the membrane which allow a transmitter fluid to be relased into the synaptic gap between neuron A and neuron B. The membrane of the neuron functions like a sieve in that small molecules and ions may pass through during this time. When the axon discharges transmitter fluid the gates open momentarily allowing many positively charged sodium ($Na+$) ions to rush into the synaptic cleft and many positively charged potassium ($K+$) ions to rush into the neuron. While at rest the membrane tends to expel the potassium ions and take in the sodium ions. When an imbalance exists at the axonal membrane, there is relaxation so molecules and ions do what they like (which is usally to move).

The synapse is not an activity, it is a place, the place of communication between one neuron and another. This communication is via chemicals which are released into the synaptic cleft when an axon "fires." The communication from only one neuron is often insufficient to trigger the action potential necessary to fire. Several excitatory inputs are usually necessary to change the balance. If a neuron receives an excitatory message on one portion of the dendrite and an inhibitory message on another portion of the dendrite, the two messages usually counteract each other. Some transmitter fluids can influence the receptive neuron with arousal while other transmitter fluids bring about inhibition.

The two main kinds of transmitter fluids identified thus far are acetylcholine, an excitatory transmitter with a positive charge, and norepinephrine, an inhibitory transmitter with a negative charge (Milner, 1970).

RECEPTORS

Receptors are glorified neurons with direct connections to the external or internal environment. They are capable of transmitting the nature of the stimulus (light, sound, smell), the intensity of the stimulus (how much light, how quiet the sound, how strong the odor), temporal duration (milliseconds or hours), and location of the stimulus (on the hand, head, or toe). Receptors are translators (transducers) in electrochemical energy and they interpret the language of the environment into the language of the body by changing one form of energy into another (sound or light into chemicals going to specific CNS areas). There is a tendency for receptors to adapt to stimuli by decreasing their own output to the CNS even though there exists continual input to them. (Hence, we cease to hear the heater blow or the clock tick, etc.) This reduces the load on the CNS (Belluzzi, 1972).

BASIC ORGANIZATION

Information is received by receptors in the eyes, ears, nose, mouth, skin, muscles, joints, tendons, etc., and sent via neurons to the brain for processing. Once a decision to act is made, neurons to the appropriate musculature are activiated and behavior occurs. Receptors and the sensory systems send messages *to* the brain and are called *afferent systems*. Motor neurons send messages *from* the brain and are called *efferent systems*. (Remember the difference by recalling that the words *exit* and *efferent* both begin with *e*.)

THE BRAIN

The brain consists of several structures, and from an evolutionary perspective, seems to function primarily to transform the patterns of sensory experience into patterns of motor response. What distinguishes complex brains from simple brains is still quite debatable but is probably related more to the complexity of interconnections of the neurons than to the size of the brain or the number of convolutions of the brain. Each side of the cerebral cortex (top cap of the brain) is divided into four lobes: the frontal lobe (in front), the occipital lobe (in back), the temporal lobe (on the side), and the parietal lobe (between the frontal and occipital lobes on top) (see Fig. 1). Under the cerebral cortex in the center of the brain is the corpus callosum and the limbic system (consisting of thalamus, hypothalamus, pituitary, and other structures). Under the cortex and to the rear of the brain is the cerebellum and coming from those structures down to the spinal cord are the pons, medulla, and brainstem. The cerebral cortex is usually thought of as a thick cap that

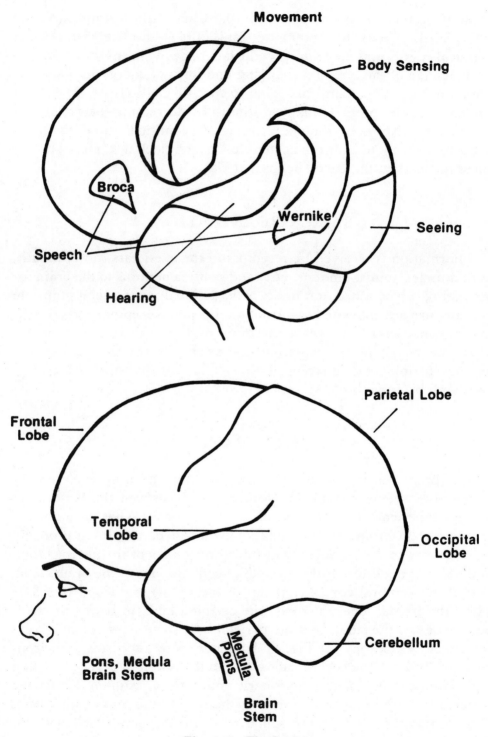

Figure 1. The Brain.

covers over all these other structures. Many smaller organs may be found in the center of the brain and to the rear, especially those of the limbic system.

Different areas of the cortex receive stimuli from different sensory systems, and the control of different kinds of behavior arise from these differing areas in the cortex. Movement and speech are dealt with primarily in the frontal lobe, including the receptors which relay information that movement is occurring and the neurons that initiate movement behaviors. Some speech is initiated in the parietal lobe as well. Body sensing is received in the parietal lobe adjacent to the motor areas of the frontal lobe. Hearing is received in the temporal lobe and seeing is received in the occipital lobe (see Fig. 1).

GOTKAV
(GUSTATORY, OLFACTORY, TACTUAL, KINESTHETIC, AUDITORY, VISUAL)

Our sensory systems develop over time and there is much debate over which system develops first. Ray Barsch (1968) believes that the infant first develops the gustatory (taste) sense, which is necessary for survival. Along with taste, olfaction (smell) is developed and the infant probably knows the smell of his mother better than the sight of his mother. Part of the feeding relationship is touch, which Barsch believes develops next. And quite early along with feeding, the infant soon learns to turn towards the mother so kinesthesia is developed. Audition develops along with kinesthesia, and finally vision improves to become the ultimate dominant sensory mode of our culture.

Another way of looking at the development of the sensory systems is through the relatively new research on humans *in utero*. From this information we have theorized that kinesthesia develops before the other senses after about four and one-half months *in utero*. Passive touch is developed at about the same time, and hearing develops just a little later. After birth, taste and smell are developed as important elements to survival. Swallowing, a vital part of eating, is mostly kinesthetic and tactual. Vision is the last of the sensory systems developed. So *our* sequence of the acronym GOTKAV would logically be KATGOV.

Humans do not see, hear, or touch, etc. some objective something that is out there. Humans *construct* a something from the stimuli and neuronal input and compare it to previous somethings they have previously experienced. With further experience and stimuli we reconstruct the something and find that the something of Day One, that was a blob then, has by Day 63, become a wood block; and further the block can be distinguished from the rubber ball (which also used to be a blob). Certainly there is something out there, but we all have somewhat different interpretations and valuings of that something. Perceiving is an interaction between each of us and the environment involving each individual's *construction of the world.*

Seeing and hearing are our distance senses, while touching, tasting, smelling, moving are employed at much closer range. It is much easier to look across the street (or around the room) to see who is there than to cross the street and touch someone's face to find out who is there. For more detailed information it is usually necessary to touch, taste, smell, and/or manipulate. For less detailed information, vision and audition are adequate.

In the more primitive animals, sensory input often results in a reflexive action, usually flight or fight (with variations). Less primitive animals have, over time, evolved a CNS that can evaluate the extent to which stimuli are dangerous or nutritious. Most sensory input will have affective values attached to it, depending on what kinds of things are occurring at any one time. Also, sensory information will have emotional coloring attached to it, not just discriminating informational components.

Evolutionary change has brought about an increase in the interaction among the sensory modalities. In humans, responses are usually based on information from all the sensory modalities. More primitive animals often rely on only one sensory system at a time. The frog only recognizes moving objects (flies) in its visual field as food, and its tongue operates with reflex flicks to trap these moving objects. Even though a frog may be surrounded by dead flies, it cannot utilize its other sensory systems to recognize the flies as food and could starve to death.

KINESTHESIA AND PROPRIOCEPTION

Kinesthesia (along with *proprioception* with which it is often used interchangeably) is probably the least understood of the sensory systems. Kinesthesia means "feeling of motion." In order to do anything with even vague success, one must be able to monitor one's movements by knowing the relative positions of different body parts in relation to each other and to gravity. This is often called the "muscle sense." It is afferent (going toward the CNS) not efferent (going out from the CNS), with which it is often confused. The receptors which comprise the kinesthetic sense are located in the muscles, tendons, and joints and are sensitive to differing qualities such as changes in muscle length, contraction, tension, or compression. The receptors in the joints are sensitive to the degree of angulation and the rate at which this angulation changes.

Proprioception is usually defined as including these sensory avenues as well as the semicircular canals in the ears which are designed to identify left from right, up from down, and front from back. There are at least six different kinds of receptors involved in sending essential information about movement to the CNS, where it is integrated to tell the individual what is happening to space/time, gravity, equilibrium, force application, mass/weight, inertia/energy. This information is usually correlated with vision, hearing, and touch and leads to a comprehensive view of the environment and one's moment-to-moment relationship with it. (Sometimes the term, proprioception, is used to include only the receptors in the ear and head and can therefore be a confusing term.)

There is also an *interoceptive sensory system* of receptors relating to pain, burning, cramping, aching, heat, cold, itch, and vibration, however we will not deal with this system in this book.

FIGURE/GROUND

Learning to sense with a focus, selecting what to include and what to omit is usually referred to as *figure/ground*. This is necessary for control and systematic data gathering. It probably develops in the kinesthetic sensory system first (Kephart, 1971) and, if lacking there, may never develop in the other systems to any extent.

Figure/ground develops in all normal sensory systems, and it is easier to explain when discussing the visual sense than when discussing the other senses. Face/vase is one example of the visual figure/ground. You can either focus on the white vase with a black background or on the black faces with a white background (see Fig. 2). You cannot focus on both at the same time. We usually focus on one thing to the elimination of other things and we do this at an unconscious level. When we are infants we are learning what to focus on and how.

When listening, it is necessary to focus on which sound you really

Figure 2. Face/Vase. From "The Interpretation of Visual Illusions," Donald Hoffman, ©December 1983 by Scientific American, Inc. All rights reserved.

want to hear: the teacher's voice or the transistor radio in your ear; the music on the radio or your mother asking you to mow the lawn; the French horns, the cannons, the harmony or the melody when you hear Tchaikovsky's *1812 Overture.*

With touch, we focus on some parts of the body surface more than we do on others. Most of us turn off information about our having clothes on; once they're on, we're more inclined to pay attention to stimuli involving the hands or mouth rather than the legs or back. But is it possible at any time to think your way around the surface of your body (*in your head? OR somewhere??*) and "feel" what kind of stimuli are impinging on the balls of your feet, shins, knees, etc., that you were *not* focused on until this particular moment, and *that* was all background to feeling the pencil in your fingers or touching your teeth with your tongue or scratching your ear.

Figure/ground development in the kinesthetic system is a little more difficult to explain. A normal person is usually in a state of *tonus,* meaning there is a little tension in all the muscles of the body. If I were to ask you to raise your hand above your head, you should feel some contraction at least in your shoulder and know that your arm is raised over your head. There is a distinct difference between resting tonus and contraction within the shoulder. The contraction in the shoulder would be the *figure* and the resting tonus of the remainder of the body's musculature would be the *ground*.

If you were diagnosed as hyperkinetic or hyperactive, one of your symptoms would be a very much increased amount of muscle tonus. Your muscles would be tense all the time and when you raise your arm over your head, the difference between that shoulder contraction and your general bodily muscular tension would not be sufficient for a clear figure/ground. You might not even know your arm is over your head. Hyperkinetic youngsters are much less apt to know where they are in space/time and often bump into things and people and have a great difficulty with perceptualmotor tasks. On the other hand, hypokinetic or hypoactive youngsters are in just the opposite boat. They have no muscle tonus and are very flaccid. When they move a body part, they use the absolute minimum amount of muscle fibers (one instead of 1000) so that, again, the contrast between the relaxed musculature and the very few muscle fibers being contracted is minimal and often insufficient for the youngster to be aware of the contraction. Hypoactive youngsters are often helped by wearing weights on their body parts (ankles, wrists, neck, etc.) so that greater contractions are necessary. Massage is often helpful in increasing tonus. Hyperactive youngsters are often helped by learning how to relax. Both hyperkinetic and hypokinetic, then, need to be carefully taught the specific kinesthetic figure/ground possibilities (Kephart, 1971).

PERCEPTUAL MATCHING

When the infant is investigating a wooden block with her eyes, it is important that she also investigate it by touching, moving, chewing, smelling, throwing, and listening to it fall so that *perceptual matching* will occur. If the infant is looking at a wooden block while manipulating a rubber ball, considerable confusion will result. Kephart calls this a *need for veridicality* while Montessori calls this *control of error:* it is an important concept throughout the learning process. In addition to perceptual matching, perceptualmotor representations will be built into constructions because of the essential manipulation and movement involved in achieving perceptual matching. Wherever possible, we should provide more than one sensory avenue of information about that which is to be learned if perceptual matching is sigfnificant.

USE OF SENSORY MODES

Our schools are primarily vision-oriented and secondarily auditory-oriented. Rarely are tactuality or kinesthesia used in the teaching method although these are probably more fundamental to human development. Structures and symbols are rarely presented except as functions of vision (as in diagrams of sentences). If a youngster is deficient in a sensory mode, it is helpful to present information to him using the deficient sensory mode and his most efficient sensory mode at the same time. And as with hand/eye coordination, it will eventually become eye/hand. This is not easy to do and takes considerable planning and creativity, particularly since most of us are not equipped to deal with kinesthesia and tactuality. If a youngster had strengths in the following order KTAV (kinesthetic, tactual, auditory, visual) instead of VATK (visual, auditory, tactual, kinesthetic), as most students are expected to, the teacher could work on presenting kinesthetic and visual material together.

PERCEPTUAL DIFFERENTIATION AND GENERALIZATION

As the infant experiences the environment and receives more and more sensory input, he begins to differentiate some things from others and develops figure/ground. Through differentiation (based on information *differences*) he can develop constructions of what is out there. As the different sensory modalities begin to make constructions about the same object, there appears to be a pooling of the information or the constructions at some level in the CNS which can elicit a common neural activity representing the object. Some call this an intersensory code or *synesthesia*. If the infant learns to differentiate square blocks visually, he will also be able to identify square blocks by touch (and with eyes closed). This is called the *establishment of a generality* and is the ability to abstract a common quality from an object and respond to it. Another example is the individual's ability to distinguish between being touched once or being touched twice and the ability to abstract the quality of singularity or duality to recognition of the difference between hearing one or two sounds, seeing one or two blocks, or moving once or twice. There is no limit to the number of generalizations (based on *information likenesses*) that can occur with such intersensory constructions. The infant develops generalizations for *ballness* and *blockness* to distinguish different groups of playthings. Hardness, softness, angledness, curvedness, smoothness, splintery: all establish *qualities of things* so that the growing individual can respond appropriately.

ACTIVITIES

1. Stand facing a partner who closes her eyes. Put each other's palms together. You lead while your partner tries to maintain contact with your hands. Reverse roles. Next do the same thing, *but* the follower keeps her eyes open and does not touch palms but visually tries to keep up without touching. Reverse leader and follower.

2. With partner, stand facing. Extend arms forward, rotate forearms so that thumbs are pointed at the ground and backs of hands face each other. Cross left wrist over right wrist so palms face. Interlace fingers, thumbs still pointed at the ground. Bring hands toward the body, thumbs leading. At this point, little fingers point to the ground and laced fingers can be observed. The second partner points at any one finger and the partner is to wiggle that finger. Try several fingers. Reverse roles. Next, the first partner should clasp her own hands and turn them inside out with her eyes closed. The second partner touches one finger at a time in scattered order while the first partner wiggles finger touched. Reverse roles.

3. With eyes closed, and partner reading, experience with all senses the following story:

   You are standing in the middle of a large valley surrounded with many craggy mountains. There is a green meadow in front of you and you are standing with your elbows leaning on a fence. Now, climb over the fence and go into the meadow on the other side. On the other side there is long grass, knee high, which you are walking through and every now and then you walk through some squishy bogs. You can smell the grass and some of the trees that are in blossom. There are many birds and deer in the meadow. Finally, on the other side of the meadow you start up the hill which is covered with shale and you need to be careful where you place your feet and concerned about whether or not the ground will hold your weight. Now you need to use your hands as the hill gets steeper and steeper. Your legs are beginning to feel the strain and your back hurts and you don't know if you will be able to make it to the top.

This should be told slowly enough so that you may *experience* (i.e., *sense*, rather than *verbalize*) the whole trip. This is just one example and many others could be used. You could take turns making up stories while the other *experiences* them and request that they use VAKTOG as much as possible. Depending on one's imagination, A, O, and G *MIGHT* have been left out of the preceding story.

4. Put your hands behind your back. Now make your hands into "tiger claws." Hold them in that position a few moments. Now, bring your hands in front and relax and put them in your lap. Did you really make your hands into "tiger claws?" How do you know that you did? This is mostly a kinesthetic activity (Ferguson 1975).

CHAPTER III

MOVEMENT AND SENSATION

INTRODUCTION

WE TALK ABOUT movement and sensation as though they are things to be looked at, sliced up, and put under a microscope. Instead, they are *processes* (not *things* which are separable) and very difficult to investigate because they really don't stand still. They flow in all directions. We suffer from the illusion that we can analyze them scientifically. The anatomical structures that make movement and sensation possible *are* things that can be looked at, sliced up, and put under a microscope, but only when they are no longer operating in normal ways.

Our language makes it difficult to keep from thinking of mind as a thing and of a body as a thing and both of them as considerably different entities. As Gunderson has pointed out, if we were to say that we do our running with our run or our swimming with our swim, we would be reasoning in the same way we do when we say we do our minding with our mind, or our thinking with our think. Minding and thinking are processes that take the whole being, as do running and swimming (Gunderson, 1971).

AFFERENT/EFFERENT

As indicated earlier, a distinction between afferent (toward the CNS) and efferent (exiting from the CNS) is usually made when describing the difference between movement and sensation. But the line is fine. Every time a body part is moved, numerous afferent receptors notify various parts of the CNS that movement is occurring, how much, of which part, how fast, at what angles, degrees of compression, tension, shearing, and torsion. Milliseconds later, visual and auditory feedback may confirm what has already been relayed kinesthetically about the movement of the body.

Since the kinesthetic neural mechanisms develop first in the embryo, all future neural input is compared and contrasted to the initial patterns that have been organized. These kinesthetic neural patternings eventually serve as referents whereby we are able to abstract such things as mass, weight, inertia, energy, force, space, and time (Meyers, 1976).

MOTOR MECHANISMS

The evolution of the CNS has essentially produced improvement in the control of movement (Belluzzi, 1972).

MOTOR STRIP

The motor strip in the frontal lobe of the cerebrum is primarily responsible for controlling discrete movements. It is the region from which most neurons (efferent) arise. Impulses from these neurons reach the motor neurons in the spinal cord either by projecting through various subcortical structures or by relaying through direct motor pathways.

The motor neuron tracts cross sides of the body near the base of the brain and therefore have contralateral control (left hemisphere controls right side of body and right hemisphere controls left side of body).

More delicate and precise movements are possible because there are more motor neurons per muscle fiber for those acts usually requiring precision (talking and writing). The mouth, tongue, and hand have a greater number of neurons per muscle fiber than the nose, back, and shin.

PREMOTOR STRIP

The premotor strip, in front of the motor strip, is specifically concerned with the acquisition of specialized motor skills and rhythmic skills. They are what Luria calls *kinesthetic melodies* because they require the gradual denervation of various parts of the movements as other parts are brought into play, creating a consecutive series of motor impulse patterns. The premotor strip usually is involved in larger, more complex movements than the motor strip (Luria, 1973).

PREFRONTAL AREA

The prefrontal area (all the frontal lobe in front of the two motor strips) has profuse connections with the other areas of the brain as well as neurons to the motor tracts. The prefrontal area is believed to be the major difference between animals and humans. Although it exists in animals, it is not as large as in humans. Motor planning or prethinking appears to occur in this area, which regulates evaluations of external impressions and directs a plan of action based on those evaluations. People with frontal lesions of any extent lose their ability to compare their performance with their original plan and they no longer notice that their actions do not correspond to the original plan. They are not aware of their mistakes and therefore cannot correct them.

It is hypothesized that the prefrontal area deals with such things as judgement, planning for the future, ambition, conscience, and abstract thinking (Milner, 1970).

It is fairly well established that the prefrontal area is the main source for programming complex motor acts (along with the motor and premotor strips) and for regulating the comparison between the actual movements and the original plan of movement patterns.

MOTOR PATHWAYS

While there are at least twelve different kinds of sensory receptors for input to the brain, there are only two motor pathways from the cortex. The pyramidal tract was the first discovered. It originates in the cortex and passes through the medullary pyramid cells enroute to the spinal cord. This tract leads primarily to the limbs, especially the hands. It is our primary tract of voluntary control.

The extrapyramidal tract was discovered after the pyramidal tract (originally thought to be the only motor system), so everything else discovered since has been labeled extrapyramidal. In general, the extrapyramidal tracts are interrupted synaptically in the basal ganglia or in the brain stem or in the reticular formation, and do not pass through the medullary pyramid cells. They are believed to carry impulses that refine and smooth out performance, and are primarily responsible for postural adjustment and rhythmic patterns.

CEREBELLUM

Acting as a sort of "futurist," the cerebellum is believed to predict the position of different parts of the body and to appraise the relationship of the body to surrounding objects. The cerebellum receives sensory input from several sources and, in conjunction with the prefrontal area, predicts the position of the limbs ahead of time and adjusts movement as change is needed.

The cerebellum plays a unique role in automating various movement patterns. When a youngster first learns to walk or when an adult first learns to boogaloo, he must use his cerebral cortex to control what he is doing or he will fall down or trip. It is necessary to use the whole frontal lobe, while the cerebellum monitors the procedure. The output cells of the cerebellum (*Purkinje cells*) at first imitate the action of the frontal lobe. They practice by modifying their connections with the frontal lobe impulses so that they are activated whenever it is appropriate. These cells memorize all of the complex muscular actions involved in each movement pattern. Given a message from the frontal lobe which has been memorized, for example walking, the cerebellum takes over and continues movement; the frontal lobe then is free to think about *where* one is walking rather than *how* to walk (Marr, 1982).

FROM REFLEXES TO GENERALIZATIONS

A reflex is a relatively constant pattern of response to a given stimulus. Most of our innate reflexes begin to function during the first six months of life. The tonic neck reflex is one of these and a difficult one to prevent. On her back, if the infant rotates her head to one side, both arm and leg on that side will extend, while the arm and leg on the other side relax, thus preventing her from rolling over onto her stomach. If the infant lying on her stomach lowers her head, it causes the arms to flex and the legs to extend. Lifting the head causes the arms to extend and the legs to flex. Along with the righting reflexes, the tonic neck reflexes assure that the body follows the head in spatial orientation.

The righting reflexes include the labyrinth reflex (keeping the head upright no matter what kind of twisting occurs in the lower body); the neck reflex (keeping the head upright if the body is tilted, ultimately causing the rest of the body to line up with head); the body reflex (when head is atilt, the body will move to be upright); and the optic reflex (orienting the head by visual control).

When pressure is applied to the palm of the hand or to the central arch of the foot, there is a grasping reflex. We are also born with sucking and swallowing reflexes and a tendency toward general body activity.

As the infant uses his reflexes in relating to the environment there is a tendency for the musculature involved to grow stronger, a tendency to repeat those things which are pleasurable, and ultimately, a tendency to override the innate reflexes. (For example, an infant must spend time and experience rolling onto her stomach to develop the musculature for creeping, crawling, and walking.) New experiences tend to be repeated for their own sake, and those repetitions lead to systems of organizing the environmental stimuli. Continuous new inputs and repetitions lead to reconstructions or more rigidly built old constructions. These are often referred to as methods of differentiation and generalization. We begin to differentiate some of our environment from other parts of it by noting differences. As this occurs we generalize about what we have differentiated (these things are suckable, those things are not suckable) noting similarities (these suckables are green, those nonsuckables are green).

Kephart (1971) described such a developmental sequence as follows: global mass → differentiation of a single movement → isolation of movement from rest of body movement (kinesthetic figure/ground) → several single isolated movements → coordinated, synchronized pattern- → several patterns → movement generalization → automation of individual movements in generalization → attention on goal of movement rather than nature of movement, hence proceed with information-gathering process.

CEPHALOCAUDAL AND PROXIMODISTAL

As an infant develops, there is a definite tendency to develop at the head end (cephalo) sooner than at the foot end (caudal). The musculature that holds and moves the head (and elements of the head, like mouth and eyes) develop sooner than the musculature that wiggles the toes and feet.

There is also a definite tendency for the infant to develop the musculature of the center of the body (proximo) before developing the musculature of the periphery of the body (distal). The musculature that moves the shoulder and elbow develops sooner than that which moves the head and fingers.

GROSS AND FINE

Another element in the developmental sequencing of maturation relates to the size of the muscles. Larger muscles develop sooner than small delicate muscles. The muscles that open and close the palm develop sooner than the muscles that contract and extend the little finger. Sometimes we demand that youngsters do fine precise skills (like writing) before they have developed sufficient strength (of hand as in holding a crayon).

MOTOR PLANNING AND MENTAL PRACTICE

How can a thought be transformed into the articulation of a word or precise purposive movement of the hand or foot? We really don't know. There are many hypotheses, but we find the most reasonable that of Georg von Bekesy (1962). He believes that if the hand is to be moved or if some words are to be said, the higher centers of the CNS transmit to a lower level an advanced program detailing how the movements are to be performed. This program is then relayed to the appropriate neurons and muscle fibers and executed. As the movement takes place, the kinesthetic receptors relay information back to the lower CNS level. If the performance and the original program are identical, no changes are made. If there is a discrepancy, then that difference will be sent to the higher CNS level where programming will be revised and corrected within milliseconds. This system reduces the load on the higher CNS level for those things that are fairly routine performances (similarities), but allows for changes if there is a variation in the performer or the environment (differences).

Some researchers refer to the original CNS program as space/time templates or subroutines and suggest that they can be stored at various levels of the CNS. Reflex patterns are thus stored in the spinal cord and brain stem; postural positions in the vestibular and cerebellar centers, and complex movement templates and subroutines in the cerebellum. The cerebrum is therefore free to devote itself to the mastery of new patterns, involving the adaptation of subroutines into new movement patterns. We can try various movement possibilities without actually moving in the CNS, before selecting the best one for the circumstances. This motor planning can be accomplished within milliseconds and is the basis of invention, organization, logic, formal operations, and abstract thought.

Initially, motor planning develops out of the infant's reflexive, repetitive behavior. As the infant begins to choose some experiences over others, he begins to plan "motorically" how to bring about the experiences he chooses (i.e., sucking and grasping). Later, when the infant sees a desired object, he must discover how to move the arm and hand (from the repertoire of movements and graspings thus far developed) in order to reach it. Still later it will become necessary to combine arm and leg movements "into a plan" to get where he wishes to go. Day after day after day, the infant improves in ability to reach, grasp, and release (crawl, walk, or use a crayon). Planning become more rapid and fluid as more and more schemes become available. At complex levels planning becomes analytical and sophisticated.

Mental practice is another phase for motor palnning at more abstract levels and involves juggling concepts into different combinations in the CNS before acting on them, as mentioned earlier.

ACTIVITIES

1. Writing

A. Write your name with your dominant hand and then with your nondominant hand.
B. Write "perceptualmotor development" with your dominant hand and then with your nondominant hand.
C. Write 7, 8, 3, and 5 with your dominant hand and then with your nondominant hand.
D. Write the word "university" upside down and backwards.

2. Balance Activities

A. Stand on right leg only. Now close eyes. How long can you stay?

B. Now stand on left leg only. Which leg is more adapted for balance?

3. Dominance Activities

A. Throw and catch balls with dominant hand, then nondominant.
B. Play badminton, tennis, or other racquet game with the dominant hand, then the nondominant hand.

Are you aware that information about most movements is available to both sides of the body? Are you aware that one side has had a bit more practice than the other side? Are you aware that you might be more ambidextrous (or ambipedextrous) than others you have seen perform?

CHAPTER IV

INFORMATION PROCESSING AND FEEDBACK SYSTEMS

INTRODUCTION

MOST OF US assume that our sensory systems "pick-up" images, sounds, models of the objects and events of the world just as they *really* are. Most of us are unaware of *raw* stimuli because we have constructed our own worlds for everything to have a place and form of recognition based on our previous experiences and constructions (Piaget).

Visual information is a pattern of excitation (light waves, particles) transmitted to the visual receptors. When we select what to focus on and what to omit (figure/ground) very little of the possible range of stimuli is transmitted at all. In addition to our constructions of the world, needs and motivations are important in determining what we experience. A hungry person looks for food, not blankets. A cold person looks for blankets, clothing, the thermostat, but not food, and so on. We select what is important to us, then we compare it and contrast it to previous experiences and constructs, and finally we construct a world of our own, a world upon which to act.

STRUCTURE OF INFORMATION PROCESSING IN THE CENTRAL NERVOUS SYSTEM

Somewhere in the CNS we have a selection system operating that determines which of the thousands of sensory receptions occurring at any one moment is important and should therefore get our attention. The information deemed important is matched with short-term memory to find out what has just happened, then it is matched against long-term memory to compare and contrast this with other experiences. If there is time, we experiment within the cerebrum, trying out different actions and thinking through their consequences before making a selection. Then we decide on the most effective response and send messages to the motor system to carry it out. Finally, we check to see if it was done correctly, and if need be, make adjustments.

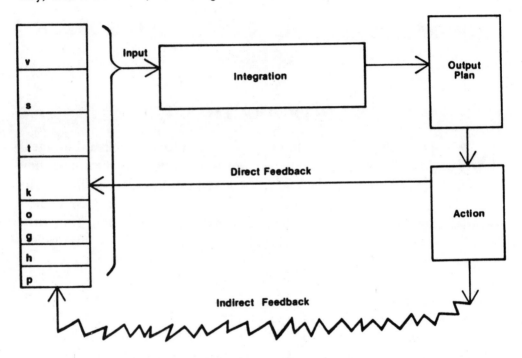

Figure 3. A Mechanical Integration of CNS.

Most people studying behavior will diagram this process with an input, an integration, and an output. Kephart would have us add the kinesthetic feedback that goes directly back to the CNS as input to make fine adjustments in our movements. The other sensory systems give us indirect secondary feedback regarding the quality of our response a bit later. So, it is possible to move and often quite effectively with just our kinesthetic system operating. This is considered a closed-loop feedback system because the efferent signals and afferent signals are all inside the body and need no external aid (as when walking a 2 x 4, blindfolded or dribbling a basketball). A closed-loop feedback system provides continuous monitoring or control and is operated by the system itself. With new integrations we get new outputs until the input and the output match, and then the process stops. Feedback in this sense means knowledge of results (see Fig. 3).

LEARNING

As a result of a lifetime of research on learning, Lashley was heard to mutter that learning was not possible because he could not find the engram (template of a memory). In his more serious moments he acknowledged that memory was probably everywhere (in the CNS), especially in the cerebrum and hippocampus (Sage, 1971).

Learning is usually considered to be a change in behavior that is relatively permanent (i.e., enters the long-term memory store). Short-term memory may last for minutes or hours. *Initial registration* refers to remembering something for about 60 seconds (long enough to dial a phone number).

Learning and memory are very closely related because of the way we define and measure learning. Both learning and memory involve the following: (1) motivation and attention, (2) initial registration, (3) short-term memory, (4) long-term memory, and (5) the unlearning mechanism by which we erase that which we evaluate as irrelevant information (Belluzzi, 1972).

An enriched environment (with perceptualmotor toys and activities) will cause laboratory animals to have significantly higher IQ than dull environments (no toys at all). The group in the enriched environment also develops better blood supplies and more acetylcholinesterase and cholinesterase in the brain. This would support the theory that synaptic activity produces these changes.

State-dependent learning involves learning to perform a task while under the influence of drugs, such as alcohol, sedatives, or tranquilizers. When the individual tries to perform the same task again — but not under the influence of the drug — he cannot necessarily perform.

Learning cannot result from electrical or chemical stimulation. One can be made more aggressive, amorous, nervous, or calm, but these methods cannot supply the perceptualmotor data necessary for learning itself. Thus brainwashing via electrical or chemical stimulation is impossible (Delgado, 1972).

A percept is a sensing of relationships (compare and contrast) between objects by locating them in space/time and observing their characteristics. Triangleness, redness, numericalness, softness, woodiness, rightness, leftness are all percepts.

A concept is based on percepts and is an organization of organizations or an abstraction of abstractions. If you have a percept of chairness and a percept of waterbedness, you might be able to combine them into a concept of waterchairness even though you have never experienced one (Kephart, 1971).

PERCEPTUALMOTOR MATCH

Initially, with the newborn, sensory information is not related to much of anything. In order to produce meaning, sensory patterns of information must become related to meaningful activities. This involves paying attention to the initial data and noticing correspondences with active exploration. As the infant manipulates the blanket, he watches his hand and relates what is being seen to what is being felt. This model of comparison is used in future explorations. He learns that a wooden block, or a cup, or a teddy bear all change visual shape as they are rotated; but he also recognizes that it is the same object known from manipulation (not vision). What could otherwise be a visual distortion becomes a standard method to learn to distinguish changes in perspective.

Held's research (1972) indicates that active exploration is necessary or distortions presented by sensory data will remain. He had subjects wear lenses that distorted their visual field (turned it upside-down). Some subjects were allowed to actively investigate their new perceptions while others were only allowed to passively observe in a wheelchair. Distortions were overcome for the first group but distortions remained for subjects of the second group. The same results were obtained with kittens raised in darkness and then allowed to see. One kitten pulled a second kitten through an environment while the second kitten was confined in a small cart. The kitten that moved itself through the environment was able to make visual sense out of the environment while the kitten that was pulled could not make visual sense of it.

When a child has a limited perceptualmotor match he will often see and hear one set of information while moving and responding in unrelated ways. Some children will be looking out the window while writing. Others will close their eyes while moving their hands to catch a ball. And others will try to learn how to tie their shoelaces while visually scanning the environment. In the above instances children will have much more success if they combine vision with tactual and kinesthetic manipulation. When a child has developed a perceptualmotor match with incoming data and motor response contributing to the same body of information, he can deal with perceptual data independently. Motor exploration is not usually necessary after one has learned this kind of matching, except when the incoming data is unclear or confusing.

SPLIT-BRAIN RESEARCH

The cerebral cortex is divided into two halves; the left hemisphere, generally responsible for the activities on the right side of the body, and the right hemisphere, generally responsible for the activities on the left side. Most of the large neurons going from the cerebrum to the arms, legs, face, torso, etc. cross over at the base of the skull causing this contralateral control. The main connection between the two hemispheres is a rather large structure called the corpus callosum.

In the 1930s split-brain operations severing the corpus callosum became popular because they diminished the hemispheric spread of epileptic seizures. Hemispheric seizures tend to mirror themselves on the opposite hemisphere which doubles the severity of the seizure. The operations were quite successful in diminishing the extent of the seizures and surgeons were surprised to find that severing this structure produced little noticeable change in the capacities of their patients other than relief from seizures.

It was not until 1951 that Myers and Sperry (Sperry, 1964) designed tests that would bring out the behavioral differences resulting from the split-brain operation. Prior tests had been of the paper and pencil variety, like IQ tests and psychological adjustment scales. Myers and Sperry tested the performance of one hemisphere separately from the performance of the other by restricting the input of information to only one side of the body. The responses varied depending on which hemisphere received the stimulus. Each hemisphere and contralateral side of the body was independent of the other.

More recent research has been accomplished using a substance called Cortical Spreading Depression which is injected into one hemisphere of a normal subject. Cortical Spreading Depression has the effect of Novacaine in that it temporarily causes a lack of function with no long-term effects. Thus far, results of this research indicate that each hemisphere tends to process information differently, producing different kinds of response abilities (*responsibilities?*).   These differences are not usually noticeable in the normal person because there is very rapid (in milliseconds) interhemispheric transmission of high-level information.

The left hemisphere/right-hand appears to deal primarily with language and mathematics and can answer questions dealing with these abilities orally or in writing. So this particular organization can answer verbal or mathematical questions with verbal or mathematical answers. Given space/time problems, however, this hemisphere has almost no ability. When asked to select a pyramid-shaped object from a bag of mixed shapes, the right hand cannot. Functioning separately, the left hemisphere cannot recognize faces nor can it define partially completed drawings or objects. It fails complex space/time tasks and complex perceptual tasks.

The right hemisphere/left-hand can respond to complex questions that can be answered nonverbally; it can respond to facial stimuli, perceive part-whole relationships, deal with complex space/time patterns, and accomplish complex perceptual tasks. The right hemisphere/left-hand is unable to give accurate spoken or written reports although short nouns can occasionally be recognized. Given appropriate letters this hemisphere can spell very simple words. With numbers below five this hemisphere can add, but it does no other form of calculation. Verbally, this hemipshere is not much better off than a three-year-old.

In the normal person, there is a time lag (in milliseconds) if information is presented to one side, requiring the response on the other side, compared to the speed with which the response could be accomplished had the information been presented to the same side as the responding side.

Our culture tends to stress the qualities of the left hemisphere/right-hand, especially in schools which are oriented toward verbal, mathematical abilities. A child whose strengths are in the abilities of the right hemisphere/left-hand encounters enormous difficulties unless presented with opportunities to solve problems in nonverbal ways. On the other hand, some youngsters who are high in verbal/math skills may be in the need of space/time problems to further develop the right hemisphere/left-hand. Dyslexics (individuals who cannot read) may have right brain bias; see things as wholes; and be unable to analyze the separate parts.

Teaching by lecturing will be comfortable for the verbally-oriented. Teaching by imitation and imagery will be comfortable for the space/

time-oriented. Perhaps both methods should be used, for both kinds of students. Perhaps more laboratory and field experiences could be used, too. The research indicates that we need a greater variety in method. Concrete examples and methods of understanding are indicated for the both kinds of hemispheric dominance.

Some who have studied split-brain research believe that the left hemisphere/right-hand person sees the world in abstractions or in bits and pieces or in details somewhat as a scientist does. The right hemisphere/left-hand person sees the world in wholeness without the attention to detail, somewhat as an artist or a mystic might.

Some world-observers have carried this a step further, indicating that the Western world is left-brain-oriented while the Eastern world is right-brain-oriented. Alan Watts (1966, before split-brain research became popular) hypothesized that the Eastern person interprets the world as whole/one, while the Western person interprets it as unjointed details. Assume the world's chaotic entanglement of stimuli appears as in Figure 4.

Figure 4. Chaotic Entanglement of Stimuli (from Watts, *The Book On The Taboo Against Knowing Who You Are*), 1966, Pantheon Books, a division of Random House, Inc.

The Eastern person accepts it as it is in all of its wholeness and reverberating patterns. The Western person cannot understand it so he puts a grid on it and studies tiny details as indicated in Figure 5.

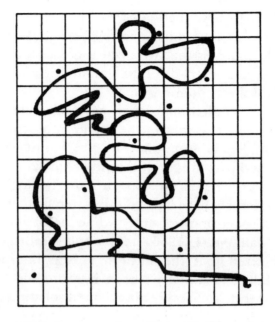

Figure 5. Western Man's Interpretation of Stimuli. (Note: dots = areas of study).

The Western person tries to put the bits and pieces together to get meaning from the world, though he is missing a great deal of it.

AUTOMATION, CYBERNETICS, AND CEREBELLUM

While driving to San Francisco several things are usually occurring at once: my ankle is extended with my foot on the gas pedal with varying amounts of pressure and relaxation as the speed needs to change, my eyes are watching the road ahead and behind, my hand is on the wheel with varying degrees of movement, my other hand is holding a hamburger and bringing it to and from my mouth while my mouth opens and closes, tastes, chews, swallows, and starts all over again. At the same time, I am listening to the radio and to my friend with varying changes in figure/ground. I am accomplishing all of these things while making appropriate adjustments for driving in rain, snow, or sleet, allowing for crazy drivers, squirrels, deer, and rocks; while computing the speed of the car, the curvature of the road, direction, wind, rate of progressive decrease or increase of speed, how fast to turn the wheel, etc.

How can a person do all of this at once, and without apparent strain? The incoming data is processed immediately and continuously while various movement programs are started by the higher CNS levels and carried out via numerous subroutines at various lower levels, especially by the cerebellum; unless something does not match or operate correctly, it is kept at subcortical levels. As circumstances change, varying amounts of attention may be directed toward those occurrences, but if all goes well and as predicted, the cerebrum is relatively free to pick and choose the focus of attention. We tend to be aware or "paying attention" only when something unusual happens.

For some youngsters and adults such subroutines are not well developed or stored. Hence, it may be necessary for them to focus attention on which part of the body to move next, and how, instead of having the freedom to think about other things. Such people will often have difficulty answering a question while walking down the street but may do well when sitting down (Barsch, 1968).

COGNITIVE STRESS

The larger the repertoire of movement patterns a youngster has, the more free he is to attend to other things. If a youngster has not developed the patterns of say, how to hold a crayon, or how to make each letter, he will have difficulty attending to *what* it is he is trying to write and will instead focus on *how* to write. The same is true of walking, running, driving, and so on.

Barsch (1968) used cognitive stress as a way to diagnose movement and cognitive problems and as a way to increase the demand that can be put on the individual. First movement fundamentals must be learned and practiced. Then cognitive stress must be added, but these additional stresses should be things that have already been learned. Examples would be crawling across the room and spelling your own name one letter to each movement, or printing your name while counting from one to ten. If these are too easy, you might spell your own name backward, or recite the Gettysburg Address, or count backward from 100 by three's, or recite poetry while roller skating around a gym. The task should not be too difficult for each individual, especially if the mechanics of either act are not well learned. The degree of stress should be increased as the individual's ability to deal with it increases, either in the motor performance or in the cognitive performance.

HOLOGRAM

A great number of people, in the 1980s, think that thinking is akin to having a little man sitting in a box seat in their heads while the eyes, ears, nose, mouth, skin, and muscles display information on something like a TV screen in the head. The little man decides what it all means and pushes the right buttons and the right thing happens. One of the more obvious problems with this belief is that the little man can only be explained by another little man in this head, and so on, and so on.

One of the more recent theories which addresses itself to a part of the mystery of how we learn/remember/think is called the hologram theory and was developed by Pribram (1971). It employs an analogy from a recent invention in physics, the photographic process of holography. If you were to photograph an object without using a lens but by using a laser beam instead, the resulting hologram would be an unusual pattern of lines or spots which would seemingly bear no relation to the object holographed. If the hologram is next viewed by means of the laser, the whole object reappears. The hologram is really an encoded version of the picture. If you were to develop a hologram on a glass plate and then shatter the plate into pieces, you could look at any piece of glass with the laser and you would see the *whole* picture. Pribram believes that the holographic process is analogous to memory because memory diffuses the picture or experience throughout the brain. Since sometimes a tiny fragment of information can trigger a whole complex memory, this may have some interesting applications (Pribram, 1971).

ACTIVITIES

1. Cognitive Stress Activities (from Barsch, 1968)

Jump rope first with right foot lead, then left foot lead, then both feet together. Pick the jumping style that you prefer and then have your partner ask you to do the following:

A. Spell your name (one letter to one jump).
B. Spell your name backward (one letter to one jump).
C. Recite alphabet backward.
D. Spell "perceptualmotor development."
E. Count to 100 by threes.
F. Recite poetry, give a synonym for each word partner gives you, sub-

tract numbers called out, add, divide, multiply, etc.

2. Arm Wrestling

A. With partner, lie down on stomach on the floor with each putting her elbow on the floor. If one has longer forearm, put a book under the shorter one so that the movements will be more even.
B. Clasp hands and when one of you says, *Go*, try to push your partner's arm until her hand touches the floor on the opposite side.
C. Were you aware of the length of your forearm? Were you aware of your grip strength? Were you aware of your ability to use leverage?
D. Try it again two or three times with each arm.

3. Leg Wrestle

A. With your partner facing the opposite direction from you and with both of you lying down on the mat, slide around until your hips are opposite her shoulders and her hips are opposite your shoulders. Lock arms.
B. On the count of one, you both kick the leg closest to the other person high in the air and adjacent to your partner. Then return your leg to the floor. On the count of two, repeat the same procedure.
C. On the count of three, kick your leg high in the air and lock your calf around your partner's calf and try to tip her over so that she does a somersault (instead of you).
D. Were you aware of the length of your leg? Were you aware of the strength in your leg? Were you aware of your ability to use leverage?
E. Try it a few more times.

4. Standing Wrestle

A. With your partner standing and with right side toward you, grasp right hands and touch the outside edges of your right feet.
B. At the starting signal, each of you will try to unbalance the other, which is considered successful when your partner moves her left or right foot (or she makes you move your left or right foot).
C. Were you aware of the length of your arm and body? Were you aware of the strength of your arm? Were you aware of the flexibility of your body? Were you aware of your ability to use leverage?
D. Try it again two or three times with each arm.

CHAPTER V

THE DEVELOPMENT OF THE FIELD

INTRODUCTION

A NUMBER OF brilliant people have played role in shaping what is now called perceptualmotor development. We will discuss just a few of those who have made resounding impressions within the field.

A BETTER WAY TO LEARN

Jean Rousseau (1712-1778) believed that civilization caused man's problems, and he developed a learning system designed to avoid civilization until one was old enough to deal with those problems. His book, *Emile,* is his blueprint of a program which describes how he would educate the boy, Emile. His first important strategy was to go back to nature. Rousseau did not believe that children were small adults and so he treated Emile as a child. He did believe that the sensory and motor systems were the instruments of our intelligence. So the first elements in his curriculum were to provide Emile with healthful conditions and all the activities in which he was interested. Rousseau felt that movement activities of one's own choice were a better way to learn. There was no instruction during this first phase of the program from ages 0 to 5. Between ages 5 and 12, Emile learned things such as swimming, leaping, and climbing *naturally* through investigation and manipulation. He ate and lived simply and by age 12, Emile was then ready to learn about learning in a more formal way.

Prior to Rousseau most educational theorists divided humans into mind, body, and spirit. Rousseau, however, did not agree and followed the belief that mind, body, and spirit are harmonious. He was the first educator to be concerned with the fact that urban institutions could be destructive. He believed that ideas arise from sensation and that knowledge, therefore, is rooted in sensory experience. His book was very well received in the new world, but in Europe several parliaments condemned it and the church burned it.

Maria Montessori (1870-1952) was the first woman to receive a doctor of medicine degree in Italy. Her first job was as directress of a school for defective children. She succeeded in bringing test scores for these children to higher levels than test scores for normal children. She differed from Rousseau in that she believed the formative period was between the ages of 0 and 6 when the child is constructing reality from experience. She also believed that children do not learn *naturally*. They need direction and guidance.

She believed that, given a wide variety of appropriate educational materials to utilize in the classroom, the child should be left to himself to make the most of his own decisions. The materials must be inherently interesting to be worthy of the student. Montessori believed children should be self-correcting and thoroughly understood by the teacher. Many of her instructional materials involved tactuality, proprioception, and movement (sandpaper letters, wooden figures, frames for buttoning clothes, tying shoelaces, variations in color, texture, weight, shape, sound, and size).

In 1907, Montessori became Directress of the Case Dei Bambini, a slum school, where her methods were just as successful. Some of the rules she applied include: (1) Each child has his own working area which is respected and not to be entered without permission; (2) If two or more children prefer to work together at any time, they may; (3) The rest of the room should be available to the child and relatively free; (4) Running, shouting, and pushing were not permitted; (5) The classroom was filled with all kinds of materials and learning activities that could be used at any time as long as things were returned in the same condition as they were found; (6) Whenever the child wished, instruction and/or assistance were available (and often the children assisted each other); (7) Teachers could introduce activities to the child, but they must never be forced upon the child; (8) Those activities available to the youngster were very carefully selected and created to lead to a mastery of reading, writing, arithmetic, etc.

Montessori's method did not spread as quickly as one might have expected, probably because she failed to inspire disciples to carry on the program and because in America, her liberal use of the word *liberty* was interpreted to mean permissiveness (when she meant responsibility).

Fortunately, Montessori now has disciples in this country, and they have very carefully striven for the perpetuation of the Montessori system. There are Montessori schools throughout the country, some in towns as small as Arcata, California, where the population is 12,500.

Jean Piaget (1896-1981) made great strides in analyzing the developmental sequences of intellectual growth. Piaget believed that the problem of knowldedge is the problem of the organism adapting to its environment. It is the same problem that perceptualmotor theorists and practitioners deal with. One constructs one's own realities and ways for dealing with the environment out of the interactions of basic biological equipment and experiences with the environment. As the environment changes and as the individual's capabilities change, so do the individual's constructions of reality. This is a circular process which ultimately results in effective ways of dealing with great varieties of environments (often called intelligence). Piaget structured his theory in terms of the chronological development of the organism, its interrelationships with the environment, and the ensuing cognitive constructs. Throughout the learning process, Piaget stressed the point that you cannot teach concepts verbally, that they must be taught through activity.

Piaget was in interactionist/constructivist. He believed that we construct our own realities out of interactions and that as environment changes, so do people.

He believed that adaptation was essential to the foregoing interactions. Adaptation can be broken down into *assimilation,* application of past experience to present, and *accommodation,* the adjustment of that experience to take account of the present (Phillips, 1975). He used the concept of development to understand that the child (not the teacher) is the main reconstructive agent in his own development.

Brief descriptions of the various developmental stages, taken primarily from the works of Phillips (1975), Richmond (1970), and Flavell (1963), follow:

A. Sensorimotor Period, 0-24 months. Beginning of cognition and academic thought.
    1. Stage 1: 0-1 month. Wired-in Sensorimotor Schemes. Grasping, sucking, gross body activity.
    2. Stage 2: 1-4 months. Primary Circular Reactions. Centered on one's own action, variations and coordination of schemes, per-

ceptual recognition of objects, pseudo-imitation.

3. Stage 3: 4-8 months. Secondary Circular Reactions. Centered on environmental consequences of body's actions (motor meaning), conservation of object, beginning of interest in relations of objects, beginning of true imitation, applying familiar schemes to familiar situations.

4. Stage 4: 8-12 months. Coordination of Secondary Schemes. Separation of means from ends, symbolic meaning. Causes outside self, beginning of play, applying familiar schemes to new situations.

5. Stage 5: 12-18 months. Tertiary Circular Reactions. Engages in *experiments,* new level of object permanence, higher level manipulation of objects, systematic variation of responses, modifying familiar schemes to fit new situations.

6. Stage 6: 18-24 months. Invention of New Means Through Mental Combination. Invention of new means through reciprocal assimilating of schemes (without excessive trial and error), new cognitive structures to apply to new situations, increased importance of internalized symbols, increased development of space/time, experimentation as *interiorized* (worked out mentally before doing), motor planning, beginning of make-believe.

7. The sensorimotor period embodies the full range of cognitive development, preoperational through formal operations, e.g., interiorized experimentation is the equivalent (and the embodied basis) of formal operations.

B. Preoperational Period (2-7 years).

1. Increasing internalization of representational actions and increasing differentiation of signifyers from significates.

2. Unique image-symbol system.

3. Preconcepts form, which are between the imaged symbol and the concept proper (the identification of partial elements with one another).

4. Sensorimotor thinking parallels symbolic activity.

5. Deferred imitations.

6. Juxtaposition, syncretism, centration, egocentrism.

7. Further development of space/time.

C. Concrete Operations (7-11 years).

1. Decentralization.

2. Language begins to operate as a vehicle of thought.

　　3. Reversibility (part-with-whole and whole-with-part).
　　4. Directionality related to viewpoint of others and viewpoint of objects or relational judgement in general.
　　5. Operations with relations.
　　6. Conservation of quantity (around 6-8 years).
　　　Conservation of weight (around 9-10 years).
　　　Conservation of volume (around 11-12 years).
　　7. Reversibility: Inversion in classes (filling and emptying a basket of beads, extending, and retracting the arm).
　　8. Reversibility: Reciprocity in relations (performing a second action which compensates for the first condition without undoing it, producing an equivalence: holds hand steady as weight is added to it, eyes move to compensate for changes in the rotation of the head thus maintaining eye contact with a particular person or object).

D.　Formal Operations (11 years and into adolescence).
　　1. Can examine one variable at a time, holding all others constant.
　　2. Learns "other things being equal."
　　3. Plane of pure possibility.
　　4. Ability to abandon own point of view.
　　5. Reversibility of thought (combining inversion and reciprocity).
　　6. Combinational system.
　　7. Combines statements about the world to produce new statements.
　　8. Can begin with possible and proceed toward real (rather than vice versa).
　　9. INRC (Identity, Negation, Reciprocal, and Correlative) groups.
　　10. Logical experiment.

According to Piaget, as one interacts, one recognized constructions or schemes. The child is the main reconstructive agent in his own development (not the teacher).

The developmental periods listed above are developmental in that the sensorimotor period must precede the preoperational period, which must precede the concrete-operational period, which must precede the formal-operational period.

Piaget has published many volumes during the last fifty years and has been the most accepted educational theorist in this country in recent years. His books are difficult to understand, but there are many comprehensible translations of Piaget.

PROFOUND DISTURBANCES OF CNS

Alexander Luria (1973) has been Head of The Neuropsychological Laboratory at Moscow University for several years. The main subjects of his studies were men who were shot, bombed, or otherwise left with brain damage as a result of World War II. He traced the functions of different hemispheric areas. He has also spent much effort connecting the role of sensation and movement in intellectual development. It was Luria who first discovered that if a person has a damaged left hemisphere, he will have difficulty with speech, but will be able to navigate pretty well. If the right hemisphere is damaged, that person should have no difficulty with speech but will have trouble dealing with space/time (Luria, 1973).

Carl Delacato (1964, 1967) has spent several years diagnosing and remediating brain-damaged youngsters. The first time we heard of the man was through an article in *Reader's Digest*. Delacato was extolled as "the person who could bring communities together." The procedure was for both parents to bring their brain-damaged youngster to his office where the child would be diagnosed. Delacato taught the parents how to remediate the problems of the youngster. Part of the remediation is what Delacato calls *patterning* which involves five people each manipulating an arm, leg, or head of the brain-damaged individual in a synchronized way. This procedure usually lasts for twenty minutes out of every sixty minutes. A new group of five adults comes in every hour, and of course, they do a lot of communicating along with some coffee drinking in between remediations. And so it was that some small towns did change their outlook on life, community, and politics. And the condition of some youngsters improved. Delacato believes that all people will do better if they develop one side of their body as the dominant side (i.e., right-handed, right-eyed, right-footed). He also developed a crawling procedure designed to provide activity feedback used as a basis to integrate the central nervous system.

A. Jean Ayres (1979) teaches at the University of Southern California and has developed nationally-used tests of the various sensory systems. She has a special interest in the innate reflexes and the difficulties some youngsters have because they cannot overcome these reflexes, most of which should disappear in the normal youngster after about six months. One of her main intervention processes is called Sensory Integration. This process is designed to utilize the vestibular system of the inner ear which greatly influences perceptualmotor development. Vestibular information is processed along with proprioception and vision in the CNS so that we can know where we are in space.

Vestibular input may be increased by rolling, somersaulting, and jumping. Proprioceptive input may be increased by crawling, pushing, and pulling. Kinesthetic impulses may be increased by carrying heavy objects and roughhousing.

READING PROBLEMS/OPTOMETRY

Gerald Getman (1970). When parents found that a child was having grave difficulty with reading, they often took the child to see an optometrist to find out why the child could not see. When the optometrist tested the child and found that she could see, both parents and optometrist (and often the teacher) were baffled. Gerald Getman was one of the first optometrists to investigate this issue. Seeing is not reading. Reading involves some additional abilities of interpreting space/time which can only come about through the development of motor coordination and directionality. Getman developed a visual-motor program to accomplish these needs. Several other researchers have followed Getman with varying kinds of programs for developing similar abilities, and for developing spatial and form organization, eye-hand coordination, tracking, tracing, etc.

LEARNING DISABILITIES

Newell Kephart (1971), who started his career in child welfare and later became a clinical psychologist at Purdue University, developed a comprehensive perceptualmotor development program designed to aid students with learning difficulties. For over thirty years, public educators have been trying to discover why some students learn less well than others and what kinds of programs will enhance their learning. Because of the work of Kephart and others, perceptualmotor development programs have become a viable approach to the problem. Following retirement from Purdue, Kephart opened The Glen Haven Achievement Center in Fort Collins, Colorado. He established an excellent program designed to evaluate students, educate parents, and instruct visiting educators on the theory and procedure. After Kephart's death in 1973, a few of his disciples established the Kephart Memorial Child Study Center at the University of Northern Colorado in Greeley. Kephart's ideas are interspersed throughout this book.

Ray Barsch (1967, 1968), a psychologist whose program was developed in Connecticut, currently conducts workshops at the University of Santa Clara and at California State University at Northridge. Both Kephart and Barsch believe that perceptualmotor development is the basis for all learning and have developed programs around this premise. Barsch called his theory *Movigenics* because of his strong orientation to movement.

PHYSICAL EDUCATION PROGRAMS

The field of physical education is considerably related to and overlaps with the study of perceptualmotor development. Yet very few physical educators have contributed to this area of study.

Bryant Cratty (1974) of UCLA has written volumes on the subject and he has drawn together considerable research data. He has developed methods for teaching spelling and math by jumping from letter to letter or number to number on "fat mats" with alphabetical or numerical grids on them. He has also worked out numerous competitions to motivate youngsters to spell and add, but his program focuses more on psychomotor than perceptualmotor development.

Jack Capon (1974) has been a physical education coordinator for the elementary schools of Alameda, California, and during the past twenty-five years he developed a practical program of psychomotor and perceptualmotor activities which he has presented via workshops and books to people throughout the country. His workshops are excellent and many participants experience a sense of accomplishment because they learn *how to do* the things they can teach their students. His is a very practical program.

CONTEMPORARY ISSUES

Mainstreaming

Recent federal legislation has provided funding for the preparation of handicapped youngsters to enter the mainstream of school life as soon as they are able. Perceptualmotor development programs are a stable part of many of these students' curricula.

Early Childhood Programs

More and more research is needed to fulfill the lack of knowledge we have for appropriate learning experiences at earlier and earlier ages. Preschool and pre-preschool programs are becoming more common. Perceptualmotor development progams are the major part of these progressive activities.

Educationally Handicapped

The term *educationally handicapped* was developed in the late 1960s and early 1970s to designate youngsters with normal or higher-than-normal IQ scores who were not learning at a competitive rate among their peers (age-mates). Programs were developed throughout the country (usually with state support) to aid these youngsters within the public school system: students commonly received an hour-a-day program which often employed elements from perceptualmotor development programs. Many such programs are still in existence although often state funding has ceased.

Master Plan

Many states supply funds for a number of different programs designed to improve particular abilities among entire school populations. Other programs tend to benefit special segments of school populations. Each school must apply separately for the funding and achieve appropriate predicted levels of performance within a prescribed time limit. Funding is often available for psychomotor and perceptualmotor programs along with many other areas of learning.

Therapeutic Recreation

Interest in the field of therapeutic recreation has mushroomed during the past five years, particularly in the development of programs for mental and penal institutions. Often perceptualmotor development activities constitute major portions of such programs because successful accomplishment is a very obvious goal. Persons active in the field believe that the basis for mental and social imbalance is frequently related to a lack of self mastery.

ACTIVITIES

Different ways of crawling is the topic of these activities (Delacato used these different forms of crawling in many of his programs.) Some theoreticians believe that each of us must go through all three of these crawls in order to develop a vertical contralateral walking pattern. Others believe that it is primarily through crawling that infants develop the strength to hold themselves in a vertical plane for ultimate standing and walking.

1. *Homologous crawling* may be accomplished by placing your hands out in front of you and onto the floor (having started in a squat position) and then by bringing your feet up near to your hands. Then place your hands forward again and bring your feet up near to your hands. This looks a bit like a bunny hop.
2. *Homolateral crawling* may be accomplished by placing your right hand and right foot forward and then by placing your left hand and left foot forward. This one will seem a bit more slithery, like a snake.
3. *Contralateral crawling* may be accomplished by placing your right hand and left foot forward and then by placing your left hand and right foot forward. Many mammals, including humans, crawl or run using this basic pattern. This method of crawling aids in developing the ability to walk.

CHAPTER VI

SPACE/TIME AND TIME/SPACE

INTRODUCTION

FOR MOST inhibitants of the western world, space and time are separate entities. These entities have external standards against which to measure amounts, form or passage (tape measure, plot map, clock, etc.). Most of us are unaware at the verbal level that space and time are two sides of the same coin which can be interpreted internally and idiosyncratically by our own constructions of reality.

Even the metaphor of a coin with a flip side continues the fallacy of separateness in space/time. Abstractions in language often misdescribe the information and world out there/in here. Most of use known (without verbalizing) if we can leap over that creek without getting wet. Most of us know if we have space/time to pass the car ahead before an oncoming car reaches us. Most of us know, about fifteen to twenty feet before we get to the curb, which leg we will use to step down from the curb.

This chapter will attempt to bring to consciousness some elements of space/time.

INTERNAL DIRECTIONALITY

As a result of movement and sensation, we begin to abstract a schemata for internal directionality. This schemata includes the coordinates for left/right, up/down, and front/back. An infant will move its head appropriately to locate its mother. It will move its eyes appropriately to locate a toy. It will turn its head in the direction of a noise, and so on. A little later, after the infant masters crawling, he will navigate about the

Figure 6. Directional Coordinates.

room stopping and investigating various points of interest. Once walking, the youngster learns to be coordinated using precise degrees of these coordinates (Fig. 6) quite fluidly and quickly.

The semicircular canals of the proprioceptive systems are essential to learning the coordinates left/right, up/down, and front/back, since each of the three canals is in one of those planes. The sensory elements of the proprioceptive/kinesthetic systems help us to know where each part of our body is in space/time.

One can survive quite well with just internal directionality as long as one does not need the cognitive structure of the verbal world. One can drive to San Francisco and have difficulty only in understanding a fellow passenger. The person who can *only drive* to San Francisco is functioning in Piaget's concrete operations. External directionality is essential for one's functioning at the formal operations level.

EXTERNAL DIRECTIONALITY

At later stages, usually around age seven, in conjunction with the social influences of school and the development of verbal thought, youngsters are able to apply their internal directionality to the external world in even more detached, cognitive ways. It now becomes possible at a particular point in time (moment in context) to look around the room and be aware that Mary is sitting to John's left, somewhat in front of Jane and behind Bob but in a higher chair than Susie's. Some people have difficulty putting verbal labels on these various positions. If they have achieved external directionality they will eventually be able to apply the appropriate words.

In internal directionality the individual is the center of her concrete operations universe. In external directionality the individual relinquishes that center and will be able to learn more about the outside world via formal operations and analytics.

BODY IMAGE AND POSTURAL SCHEMA

Many theorists use different terms for what we are here referring to as internal directionality and external directionality. The most common variations are *body image* and *postural schema*. In the 1920s Henry Head, a British neurologist, was probably the first to organize a comprehensive theory of body image. He used the term *schema* to represent the model that each person constructs of himself. This model is the standard against which all body movements and posture are judged. He felt that movement would be impossible without such a concrete structure. He thought most of the functioning of the schema was unconscious and served as a frame of reference for evaluating the wide range of individual experiences.

BARSCH'S NEAR, MID, FAR, AND REMOTE SPACE

Barsch (1968) believes there is a "spatial expansion process" that occurs as the individual becomes more and more competent.

Near space is within arm's reach. Barsch believes this is the most desirable space zone since it involves the highest level of trust. The infant is involved with its fingers, toes, its immediate here/now. It can expand near space to include those things that are reachable (a crib kid).

Mid space is just beyond reach, around four to twenty feet away. This becomes important as the infant learns to locomote (crawl, walk). As the space one investigates gets larger so do the sensory constructs of space/time, the world grows along with the youngster (a house kid or yard kid).

Far space involves twenty feet and beyond (a school kid). When the individual can accomplish complex, concrete space/time sequences sufficiently to get to and from school, store, playground, etc., the individual is a school kid.

Remote space can extend all the way to infinity (an adult). The further out in space one is, the less precise the detail. There is a greater need to tolerate ambiguity and to use abstraction.

Barsch's *expansion of space* is developmental and entails trusting youngsters to deal with less and less concreteness and more and more formal operations. There is a tendency for each individual to be more comfortable in one specific space zone. Barsch believes that near space people live in the here/now, are most interested in detail, do not like uncertainty, and are the people who end up getting the job done. He thinks that mid space people tend to live in a valley of alternates and want all the evidence before making a decision. They often lead lives of indecision unless they find a guide to direct them. Far space people tend to postpone the now and are concerned with the future. They avoid detail but enjoy planning. Remote space people are our visionaries who are concerned with infinity, truth, and philosophical questions. They are often master planners or disoriented schizophrenics.

Barsch believes the the whole of mankind is balanced by the distribution of all these space people. We learn details, decision making, planning, and how to expand for future goals, and hopefully we are able to deal effectively with all four zones.

THE TIME IN SPACE AND THE SPACE IN TIME

We are always some place at some time (Barsch, 1968). Time can be interpreted as a space interval:

rhythmic times $=$ "/"/"/"/"////'////'////'

and space can be interpreted as time interval:

San Francisco is six hours away by car.

Einstein's theory of relativity includes the determination of a planet's distance from the earth by time measurement. Most psychologists believe that when one loses his sense of place or time (or identity), he is psychotic.

Each of us is the center of our own universe and it is important to know where/when that is. "I'm where it's at." We all have a different "at" which fluctuates with time so it is important to develop one's own center.

TIMING

In complex situations the timing phase of space/time may become more crucial and is often referred to as "timing" though it is actually space/timing. If I pass the basketball twelve feet in front of my teammate at a rate of 40 mph, while my teammate is moving toward that spot at a rate of 20 mph, he might not be at the right space/time to catch the ball. An opponent might be there instead. When I drive down the road at 55 mph and try to judge the speed of an oncoming car 500 yards ahead of me, accuracy is critical when I am passing, so I can't operate in infinite space/time.

READING AND SPACE/TIME

Reading is a space/time task which requires the ability to project one's internal space/time out onto the external world. In attempting to read the word *SAW* it is necessary to move from left to right and look at the *S* (and know it isn't a *Z*), before looking at the *A* (and know it isn't a *V*), before looking at the *W* (and know it isn't an *M*). Telling *d* from *b* requires a left/right orientation. Telling *p* from *b* requires an up/down orientation. If one's internal space/time is faulty, or if one has not learned to apply it externally, one will not be able to distinguish

d from *b*

q from *p*.

MATH AND SPACE/TIME

Mathematics is also a space/time task and involves the relationships between objects and details. How much time and space is involved in walking to the door? What degree of angulation and force must be used? When I reach for a glass, how long and far do I reach? How much pressure do I exert, and over what length of time, in order to grasp the glass sufficiently so it does not drop or break?

When playing a "simple" game of tennis, each time you plan to return the ball it becomes necessary to compute at some level the speed of the ball; angle of flight; the curvature of fall; direction; rate of progressive decrease of speed; wind; spin; effects on the ball's bounce; how fast and in what direction to run; when to turn your side to the net, start the backswing, and shift weight in order for the strings of your racket to intercept the ball. All are mathematical computations in space/time. The same complexity and necessity for computations exists to some extent for every movement.

ACTIVITIES

1. Jump Rope (or run-in-place) for Time

Jump rope with your back to the clock for twenty seconds while partner says when to start and stop. Next try to jump rope for twenty seconds without looking at the clock. Your partner should advise on accuracy. Reverse roles. (Second person should perform better because she had time to develop a strategy for space/timing.)

2. Tumbling Progression

A. Log roll
B. Forward roll
    1) Kneel to sit
    2) Squat to squat
    3) Stand to stand
C. Backward roll
    1) Roll back and elbow stand
    2) Squat to squat
    3) Stand to stand
D. Head stand
    1) Tripod
    2) Stand
E. Cartwheel
F. Dives
    1) Over one flat body
    2) Over one kneeling body
    3) Over two flat bodies
    4) Over two kneeling bodies
G. Hand stand
    1) Head up
    2) Back straight.

CHAPTER VII

BALANCE, LOCOMOTION, RHYTHM

INTRODUCTION

IN ADDITION to developing figure/ground, directionality, and space-timing (discussed in Chapters II and VI), there are several other qualities that must be developed in the process of acquiring the capacity for formal thought. These include balance and gravity, locomotion, rhythm, manipulation, pediculation, relaxation, and body concept. This chapter will deal with balance and gravity, and locomotion and rhythm.

BALANCE AND GRAVITY

Gravity, often referred to as the last remaining constant on this planet (some say even this notion is changing), must be addressed if one is to investigate one's surroundings. It involves developing a state of stability or equalization of the body parts about the central vertical pull of gravity. As the body moves, the center of gravity also moves. In Eastern cultures this center of gravity is called *Ki* or *Hara*. Whether in the East or the West, for the individual who is standing motionless, the center of gravity is located about an inch or two below the naval. In motion it becomes necessary to change the varying relationships of the body parts relative to this gravitational pull in order to avoid falling over. This process involves all movements and involves stabilizing one part of the body (such as the left leg) while another part (the right leg, as in walking) is in motion. When you are sitting in a chair writing, the legs and trunk need to be stabilized so as to avoid falling off the chair and also in order to free the dominant hand for fluid writing movements.

It takes considerable experience for the infant to stabilize so that he can reach for something in his crib, even though most of the body rests upon the mattress and therefore has a wide base of support. At a later stage of development the infant will learn to support himself on four points (hands and knees). Progressively, beginning with crawling, he will learn to allow one or two of these support bases to be moved while the others stabilize. Once the infant has become proficient with crawling, which then becomes increasingly bipedal (or *two-pointed* as two bases move while the other two stabilize), the youngster becomes ready to stand (still bipedal, on two feet). With some experience in upright balancing on two feet the infant will begin to experiment with unipedal (one point) balance as he stabilizes one foot and moves the other forward. From the time the infant stands (usually between 11-13 months) until the time he develops a stable, fluid, rhythmic walk, three years of effort will have elapsed. The balancing equations involved here must occur in all the space/time coordinates.

These balancing constructions make it possible for each individual to maintain a flexible orientation to a changing environment. The center of gravity is related to directionality development, coordination of cross-lateral movement, exertion, relaxation, and stabilization.

The person who cannot answer complex questions while walking, but who can while sitting down, has a balance problem. Kephart hypothesized that one of the main sources of this problem is that youngsters are forced to walk too soon. When a youngster develops the musculature and balancing constructs of space/time, inertia/force/energy, gravity/weight/mass, he will begin to learn to walk on his own. Our culture seems to push parents into believing that if a youngster doesn't walk by 12 months of age that he is slow. Therefore, there is a tendency for parents to push walking before the youngster is ready. Many youngsters will even succeed in walking but it may be at the cost of total attention to the process.

Such a child won't be able to see where he is walking nor will he be able to take in important "passing" information as he travels because his total attention will be on *how* he is walking. This type of youngster will continue to give total attention to the process even after sufficient coordination and musculature have been developed. He will not have developed space/time, inertia/force/energy, and gravity/weight/mass very effectively. He will either need to be taken back to ground level (lying, sitting, crawling) where balance constructions are not so essential, and be carefully taught to experience gravity and balance, or he will need new, novel, unusual, or perhaps scary experiences (trampoline, swimming, flyaway, earth ball) that will affect him sufficiently and in such a way that new constructions will be created.

A number of studies show high correlations between balance beam walking and other balancing activities and reading. But learning balance beam walking in itself does not usually aid reading. A whole series of balance movement patterns (instead of splinter skills) is necessary to bring about the balancing-related cognitive constructions.

HUNT AND JONES STUDY OF AUTISTIC CHILDREN

Hunt and Jones (1967) worked with so-called "hopeless" autistic infants in a unique circumstance. One of the elements they thought might be missing in the lives of these infants is related to several PMD constructs. Hunt and Jones believed that these infants had little interaction with others their own age, somewhat in the sense that puppies and kittens would normally have with littermates. For six months infants were put in a small room, allowing one and one-half square feet per infant, for 20 minutes a day. They were observed for 20 minutes preceding this event, 20 minutes during the event, and 20 minutes following. Social relationships were particularly observed, and the researchers found a significant improvement in sociability among all of the infants. While in the small room the infants could not keep out of each others' way. When one infant prodded another in the stomach, the poked baby learned to resond in a number of ways. When an infant screamed in the ear of one of the others, the second infant responded vocally most of the time. These infants were forced to deal with balance and social closeness, both of which caused more structured, informed responses to their environment.

GRAVITY ACTIVITIES

Bobath and Bobath (1975) developed a technique for use with blind youngsters which has been quite effective with all kinds of youngsters. It involves placing the youngster on a rocker as in Figure 7. The rocker should have a carpeted top that is larger than the youngster. While the child lies on the rocker she should be rocked gently in order to feel the pull of gravity and changes in the center of gravity as she goes back and forth. The internal organs are moved back and forth and it is this movement which teaches the youngster up-down, front-back, right-left. Wives tales about rocking chairs happen to have a basis in this instance because they coincide with movement of muscles and internal organs as the individual learns about space/time, energy/mass, etc.

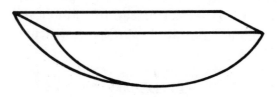

Figure 7. Rocker.

LOCOMOTION

Splinter Skills (Specificity) vs. Patterns (Generality)

"A splinter skill is a performance learned in a specific manner to satisfy a specific need or demand. It is performed with high degrees of skill but with a minimum of flexibility" (Kephart, 1971). Many athletic skills are splinter skills (psychomotor motor skills).

The youngster whose total attention is on walking is an example of a person whose walking is a splinter skill. Kephart would provide as much variation as possible in learning any skill so that it is flexible and can be performed in a number of different ways, depending on the circumstances. When splinter skills are learned, they are very specific to a narrow stimulus. When movement patterns are learned there is the freedom to use them in a number of different settings. The youngster who has developed a walking movement pattern can walk down the sidewalk, walk on the lawn, walk up a trail with a back pack on, walk at the beach, and so on.

MECHANICS

Locomotion involves stabilizing one leg while moving the other forward in a thrusting motion. It can be thought of as losing one's balance and then regaining it. It is necessary to have a construction that deals with this ever-moving center of gravity in order to keep enough support under it to stay upright. Arm rotation is in opposition to leg rotation because it is easier to stay stable.

DIVERSITY

In addition to all the ways of locomoting (walking, running, leaping, hopping, skipping, jumping, and galloping) there are a number of ways to provide variation and diversity in order to arrive at locomotive movement patterns. Barsch and Kephart would include the following variations:

large steps	pigeon-toed
small steps	duck walking
tiptoeing	backwards
tromping	sideways
walking on heels	sideways with crossover
uphill	between rungs of ladder
downhill	between tires
in sand	on foam rubber
on stepping stones	on cement
on grass	in water
on sandpaper	on gravel
on ice	etc., etc.

Barsch would add cognitive stress once youngsters could accomplish the preceding smoothly.

RHYTHM

Rhythm is defined in a number of different ways. It is believed to be developed out of each individual's own biological rhythms, such as heartbeat, breath rate, blink rate, the rates at which hormones enter the blood stream, etc. Rhythm does seem to involve a sense of time.

Kephart believes that we have three kinds of rhythm: (1) a motor rhythm which is an ability to perform a series of movements with a consistent time interval, (2) an auditory rhythm which involves recognizing equal temporal intervals between auditory stimuli (as in singing, dancing, or listening), and (3) a visual rhythm involving systematic exploration of visual space which is too extensive to be taken in in one fixation (looking around room, reading, etc.).

PROPRIOCEPTIVE MOTOR-PLANNING

Perceived rhythms include the perception of any temporal or spatial ordering in the environment. It is perhaps most easily dealt with through one's own proprioceptive motor patterning since that is internal and can be adjusted to one's own desires or needs. Once this internal construction of rhythm is established (such as allowing one to express whatever rhythm he is feeling), it will be eaiser for him to interpret external rhythms.

ACTIVITIES

1. Walking. Walk around the room, lawn, playground using the Barsch/Kephart variations above (Barsch, 1968 and Kephart, 1971).
2. Roll down a mat which has a distinguishing center line and keep your belt on that center line until you reach the other end of the mat. Barsch believes this helps to organize one's capacity for directionality and is excellent for learning the mechanisms of walking.
3. Metronomic activities (from Barsch). Have a partner beat out some kind of rhythmic beat (not too fast and fairly regular) with a pencil or a drum or use a metronome while you respond with eight beats of each of the following:
   A. Blink
   B. Wink right eye
   C. Wink left eye
   D. Scrunch nose
   E. Open-close mouth
   F. Hunch right shoulder
   G. Hunch left shoulder
   H. Hunch both shoulders
   I. Breathe in and out
   J. Bend right knee (keep foot on floor)
   K. Bend left knee (keep foot on floor)
   L. Bend both knees (keep feet on floor)
   M. While lying on the floor, move right arm from side of body, slid-

ing over floor until the hand is above the shoulder (on floor)

N. Move left arm from side of body, sliding over floor until the hand
is above the shoulder (on floor)

O. Alternate J and K

P. Alternate M and N

Q. Do J and M together

R. Do K and N together

S. Do J and N together

T. Do K and M together

U. Alternate doing J and N, and then K and M.

CHAPTER VIII

MASTERY

THE IMPORTANCE of developing effective control over the physical self, and eventually the environment, cannot be overstated. Efforts toward "connectedness" with understanding of the world are dependent upon manipulative/investigative control. A belief that we are the masters of our fate is vital to total well-being, at least in Western culture.

MOTORPERCEPTUAL CONTROL

Since kinesthetic receptors develop first *in utero* with movement, they lead the other sensory systems into their own independence. Initially, with infants, the hand finds the wooden block which is then processed by the other systems through chewing; touching; visual inspection of surfaces and angles; listening to it land; etc. Situations where the hand is the first involved are called hand/eye control (Kephart, 1971). In walking, initially, the foot finds the floor and the eye follows what the foot is doing. This is called foot/eye control. The body moves and then the senses take in what becomes available. This is called body/eye control. Such situations should properly be called motorperceptual control. Later, after many experiences with movement as initiator, the sensory systems begin to pick up points of interest to be investigated *and the body follows*. The eye finds the wooden block and the hand picks it up. The ears hear the big ball bounce across the room and the body moves toward it. These are called eye/hand, eye/foot and eye/body controls. They could also be labeled ear/hand, ear/foot and ear/body controls.

REACH, GRASP, RELEASE

When the child makes contact with objects in the environment three steps occur: reach, grasp, and release (Kephart, 1971). *Reach* involves movement of the body and arm so that the hand is brought in contact with the object. *Grasp* involves the actual holding of the object (or a part of it) while manipulating it. *Release* involves letting go, and often, losing interest. These are important skills for the development of information about the environment and must be used effectively in relation to each other. If one were to grap and release before reaching one would never really make contact.

GIVING FORCE TO OBJECTS

Often when releasing an object (in the process described above) force is given to the object causing it to be moved some distance, rather than just being dropped. This is the beginning of throwing. When a youngster is not pleased with the presence of some object he will learn to push it away. Still later he will learn more refined ways to exert force on it by hitting, kicking, etc.

RECEIVING

A more difficult skill is that of receiving force because receiving force involves more space/time constructs than producing force. Catching is the most common of these receiving skills, but receiving skills also include trapping, interposing, kicking, or volleying a moving object; or falling (as in falling from a train). Initially it is easier to learn to receive gentle pushes than to receive fast moving balls.

The important point in developing receiving skills is to reduce the speed of the moving object as gradually as possible. When we rigidly expect moving objects to stop all by themselves, we have a very painful meeting with the object, in the extreme to the point at which the object would break. When catching a ball it helps to reach out for the ball and pull it into the body immediately. When jumping off a train a series of somersaults would be much preferred to jumping and landing on both feet.

IMPLEMENTS AND APPARATUS

Skills using implements and apparatus are more advanced than those without implements and apparatus. A ten-year-long implement progression in games might include (1) learning to bounce balls with the hands, (2) throwing balls, (3) intercepting balls, (4) hitting moving balls, (5) playing handball, (6) playing racquetball, (7) playing tennis, and (8) batting a softball. The implement gets larger and further from the body. Different, more involved constructions are necessary for each step. The farther the contacting surface is from the body the more abstract the construction.

Apparatus usually involves gymnastic equipment: jungle gyms, rings, see-saws, balance beams, stegels, horizontal bars, parallel bars, vaulting boxes or horses (bench, couch, tree limbs, etc.). Each piece of apparatus needs to be learned differently. A vaulting progression might start with vaulting over a bench, then a couch, then a low 4 x 4, and finally a vaulting horse or a stegel. Again the underlying constructions get more and more complex as the apparatus gets higher and less flexible.

INTERCEPTION

Interception is different from simple catching and involves bigger spaces, faster objects, etc. Interception is one of the most difficult skills because it involves creating constructions to determine the speed, angle of flight, curvature of fall, direction, rate of progressive decrease, etc., of the object before one is able to move to the right place/time. With faster-moving objects there is less time to determine all of the necessary computations, and hence there is more difficulty intercepting them than intercepting slower-moving objects.

MOVING IN RELATION TO SELF OR OTHER BODIES

Moving one's whole body in relation to someone else is even more complex because an individual does not often know the intent, strategy, or subtleties of other bodies.

Self

Moving anywhere anytime without regard for other people or objects is the easiest and freest form of movement.

With

Moving with other bodies by mirroring them or in dance situations where movements can be preplanned is the easiest way to move with another person.

With, But. . .

With, but is another movement possiblity wherein the individual builds toward a more synchronized relationship. Examples include early dance or swimming relationships; driving a car and keeping to one side of the road while others keep to theirs; walking down the street with a four-year-old brother and eight-year-old sister.

Without

Moving without other bodies, in an attempt usually to be rid of another body is more difficult. Examples include basketball, soccer, football, etc. In order to be successful, individuals must learn to "fake out" opponents by false moves and they must also learn to read opponents' "fake out" attempts.

Against

Moving against other bodies in an effort to overcome their strength, speed, or flexibility can be difficult and involves constructions related to leverage, force, gravity, mass, weight, energy, etc. Wrestling and boxing are the most obvious examples of this kind of sport.

PEDICULATION

People in this country generally have more difficulty with activities involving foot movements than do people in countries where soccer is popular. Learning to kick and intercept moving balls with the feet is somewhat similar to catching or volleying moving balls with the hands.

People in this country simply have not had much experience developing foot coordination.

RELAXATION

Relaxation is important to consistency and endurance. Tension can cause loss of fluidity; it can tire a person rapidly; and it can reduce power. Many youngsters with learning difficulties are overly tense and often need to be taught how to relax. The two most common relaxation programs employed in schools are Jacobsen's technique and Edgar's technique.

Jacobsen's technique can be used with several youngsters at the same time, while Edgar's requires a one-to-one relationship. (Edgar's technique is used less frequently of the two, though it undoubtedly produces the greatest degree of relaxation.)

Jacobsen's technique can be employed by the individual when he is in need of relaxation because it is easy to take home when school is over. It is based on learning the difference between tension and relaxation within one's own musculature (Jacobsen, 1938).

DEVELOPMENTAL PROGRAM SEQUENCE

The developmental program sequence below was designed to move from least difficult to most difficult in terms of developing movement constructs for efficient performance. As you read, consider your own learning progression.

Group A

1. Manipulation of objects
2. Movement in relation to self
3. Relaxation
4. Basic locomotion
5. Rhythmic activities

Group B

6. Swimming
7. Tumbling
8. Trampoline

9. Elementary track and field
10. Elementary gymnastics
11. Movement exploration

Group C

12. Throwing and kicking
13. Interception (Catching and kicking moving objects)
14. Wrestling
15. Team games

Individuals should develop Group A activities before they develop Group B, and they should develop both Group A and Group B before attempting Group C.

ACTIVITIES

1. Relaxation (our version of Jacobsen's (1938) technique). Read the following two pages to a partner, then ask the partner to read them to you.
   A. Lie down on your back and relax as much as you can with arms at sides and legs out straight. Feel yourself sink into the floor.
   B. Clench the fist of your right hand and tighten all the muscles clear up to the shoulder. Feel what it feels like. What does tension feel like? Now relax the whole arm and feel what relaxation feels like. Feel the difference between tension and relaxation. Repeat this procedure three times.
   C. Clench the fist of your left hand and tighten all the muscles clear up to the shoulder. Feel what it feels like. What does tension feel like? Now relax the whole arm and feel what relaxation feels like. Feel the difference between tension and relaxation. Repeat this procedure three times. Now go back and check your right arm and be sure it is relaxed also.
   D. Tighten the muscles on top of the right foot by curling the toes upward (or tighten the muscles on the bottom of the foot by pointing the toes if you are sure the calves of your leg will not cramp) and contract all the muscles of the right leg clear up to the buttocks. Feel what the tension feels like. Now, relax the whole leg and feel what relaxation feels like. Feel the difference between tension and relaxation. Repeat this procedure three

times. Now go back and check your right and left arms and be sure they are still relaxed.

E. Tighten the muscles on the top of the left foot by curling the toes upward and contract all the muscles of the left leg clear up to the buttocks. Feel what the tension feels like. Now relax the whole leg and feel what relaxation feels like. Feel the difference between tension and relaxation. Repeat this procedure three times. Now go back and check your right and left arms and your right leg to be sure they are still relaxed.

F. Much of our tension is expressed in our breathing so now simply feel yourself breathe. Feel your lungs inflate and deflate. Feel the air rush in and out your nose and/or mouth. Notice that you are probably breathing high up in your torso. Now try abdominal breathing. This involves inhaling down deep into your abdomen so that your stomach rises when you inhale and falls when you exhale. Try breathing in one very deep breath while your stomach slowly rises and then exhale very slowly while your stomach slowly lowers. Repeat this three times very slowly.

G. (Jacobsen believed that much of our thinking involved talking to ourselves and that if we are to relax we must stop talking to ourselves.) So now count to ten slowly and loudly and feel what tension you can in your lips, tongue, and voice box. And when you are through counting, feel what relaxation you can in those same areas. Next, count to ten by whispering slowly and clearly and feel the tensions in the speaking apparatus. Feel what relaxation you can when you are through counting. Next count to ten without moving your lips and feel the tension that even this causes. Feel the relaxation in those areas when you are through. Check your right and left arms and right and left legs and breathing apparatus and be sure all are still relaxed.

H. (Jacobsen also believed that we often think through visual imagery, so our visual apparatus needs to be relaxed if we are to stop thinking.) Close your eyes very tightly and feel all the tensions this creates around your eyes. Now relax and feel what a great difference relaxation makes. Repeat three times. Now go back and check your right and left legs, breathing apparatus, and speaking apparatus and be sure they are still relaxed.

I. Now, if you're not completely relaxed or asleep, start this whole procedure all over again with A and continue through H or until you reach complete relaxation. Most people succeed in relaxing before they have gone through the procedure twice.

J. This is a technique that should be mastered so that you do not have to be lying down, or counting to ten out loud or tightly closing your eyes. The idea is that you should be able to use this in a number of situations: when you appear for a job interview, when the boss criticizes you, when your mate yells at you, when your child bites your toe, etc. This is a technique that should be with you at all times so that you can relax instead of getting high blood pressure or an ulcer. Students need it so that they can carry on even while having difficulty with multiplications at the blackboard, while trying to solve a difficult conceptual problem, or while having reading problems within a new book.

CHAPTER IX

BODY CONCEPT AND SELF WORTH

INTRODUCTION

A S WE INTERACT with the significant people in our lives, we develop feelings of adequacy or indadequacy depending upon the acceptableness of ourselves and our bodies. Later the abstract abilities of our bodies and selves will continue to contribute to and overlay these initial feelings of worth.

Body image is a term usually defined as an *unconscious,* Freudian construct of body valuing which can only be measured through the use of projective techniques (Fisher and Cleveland, 1958).

Body concept is a term usually defined as an *aware valuing of the body* which can be measured with more obvious, conscious, open techniques. Both terms are often used and misused interchangeably.

DEVELOPMENTAL

The body is the first self concept. It is always the only tangible part of the self. One can conceal most things except for one's body and movement. The first impact one makes on others is through the appearance and movement of the body.

For the most of a person's life, especially as an infant, he is a part of his mother's body concept and usually to a lesser degree, his father's body concept. If the parents are reasonably secure people, comfortable with who they are and what they can do, they will extend that security and comfort to the child. If they are insecure, however, they will project insecurity onto the child.

As the infant experiences the environment and constructs his own reality, he begins to develop a feeling of self mastery. Being able to reach for and locate a rattle, a block, a toy is most joyous and becomes even more so when he can also hold onto it and manipulate (chew, touch, smell, throw) it in some way. Self mastery becomes a delightful end in itself and most of the possible manipulations will be repeated over and over, beyond mastery. Learning to walk, talk, tie shoes, button a shirt, ride a trike and then a bike, are all activities that impart a sense of accomplishment. However, the more difficulty an individual encounters during the learning process and the more he is made to feel like a failure, the more he will come to devalue his body.

When a girl is born she is treated as *a girl* from the moment she arrives. And a boy is treated as *a boy*. The girl will be looked at and talked to more than her brother. She will be touched and handled more than her brother. She will not be encouraged to explore, be independent, and master the world as will her brother. She will be allowed more freedom of emotional expression while her brother will be allowed more freedom of physical expression.

As youngsters grow up, physical abilities are quite important to both sexes: winning/losing races, contests, or fights; being chosen first/last for a team (a most inhumane way to pick teams) are all quite important. Later, as youngsters approach puberty, physical activities become more important to boys while for girls physical appearance takes on importance. Aside from sports and games the manipulative abilities of putting together a dress or a motor, a vacuum cleaner or a motorcycle are quite important to our sense of accomplishment. Driving a car, swimming, and dancing can be important to both sexes.

Typically, as they approach (and pass) puberty, girls become less functional than boys in their use of movement. For instance, the way a girl walks depicts one of the ways in which she defines her own sexuality. In some ways, the less functional the walk, the more sexual the walk.

Before a daughter or son starts school, most parents have made an attempt to ensure that the youngster has to some degree learned the appropriate sex role. If parents have failed in this, most teachers will ensure that it occurs.

Before a girl completes elementary school she needs to know how to avoid sexual *difficulties*. In general this refers to being aware of what she is doing and what it *means* to other people, and also gaining awareness of what other people are doing and what it usually *means*. Girls are taught to look for and expect ulterior motives more than boys. As girls mature they are taught that their sexuality and individuality are one and the same thing. *Nice* girls *are not* openly promiscuous but they *are* sexual (a difficult line to draw).

Often a person will attribute a goodness or a badness to a body part or function, usually reflecting parental or peer approval or disapproval. Badness is more apt to be connected to the genitalia and sexual functioning, or to parts of the body that either (1) don't perform up to some standard, i.e., the left hand or foot, or (2) don't look quite right, i.e., large nose or ears, small penis or breasts. Goodness usually becomes associated with the parts that are approved of as especially attractive. Most of us are aware of more badnesses than goodnesses. In some instances people disown the bad elements. In more extreme circumstances of schizophrenia, people often *lose* a body part (it is just missing even though someone else can see it) or they are unable to orient in space and time. Sometimes a schizophrenic cannot tell right from left (Schilder, 1950).

Some studies of juvenile delinquents indicate that a significantly high percentage of them have serious deficits in perception and verbal skills. Because of failures related to mastery and body concept these youngsters have been losers all their lives, with little hope of becoming successful at anything (Kephart, 1971).

DISTORTIONS

Body concept is usually distorted to some degree by several elements of our culture. Appearance is probably most damaging to the individual because it bears no actual relationship to effectiveness of function. Social customs, values, and the media dictate beauty, handsomeness, homeliness, etc. Unfortunately, even those who are deemed attractive in most ways are made aware of those elements that are not as attractive as they could be. So even attractive people find things about their bodies to feel bad about. Hair and clothing styles are most conformed to during high school years, but there will be considerable divergence after high school, particularly among those individuals who go to college. There exists a strong tendency at most ages to need to appear in clothing that is appropriate to our roles.

One element that often leads to insecurity is the changing nature of the human body. We are either growing up or growing old. As we grow up we are never sure what we will attain. Also growing up often causes insecurity because one doesn't really know whether he will become fully male or female until maturity. It is impressed upon us as extremely important. In growing old we are never sure what we will maintain. Growing old is usually more traumatic for women than men because of women's identity as sexual objects. (In this culture old women are not sexual.) As awareness of aging approaches, anxiety increases. It might start with the plucking of the first grey hairs or the taping of the first *real* wrinkles, or with jogging and exercise programs, but somewhere along the way it finally sinks in that the aging process has begun. Thoughts of losing one's mate or not finding a new one become prevalent because the individual senses she is losing her sexuality and identity at the same time. (Fortunately, many learn that it is possible to develop a different sense of sexuality and a different sense of identity that may be even better than the first.)

Masculine and feminine body shape stereotypes can also cause the individual to question acceptability. Women with small breasts and men with small penises are thought to be less adequate sexually, even though size has little relationship to sexuality. Total size of the body is another complication. Studies (Jones, 1949) indicate that men who grow tall sooner are better adjusted socially than men who grow tall later, even though the two groups may end up the same height. Women who grow tall sooner are less well adjusted socially then women who grow tall later even though they up the same height. It appears that in the formative years, just before and during puberty, we each form a fairly stable concept of where we fit into the sex/role, social/role "pecking order" and we maintain that identity even when the physical relativity has ceased. Subjects in Jones' research, interviewed at age thirty-five, were found to have maintained the same social adjustments at maturity as they had established in junior high school.

Men with narrow shoulders and large hips are often ridiculed, as are women with broad shoulders and narrow hips. Men are supposed to be tall and women short, so those of us who don't fit these stereotypes experience some added trauma.

Women more than men are allowed and encouraged to construct a facade so that they will *look* the role of sex objects. Only recently have men been indulging in such things as hair transplants, face lifts, sexy clothing, padded jock straps, and the chorus-line antics of disco exhibitions and singing groups.

By the time we are adults we have pretty well established which fa-
cades we prefer and which roles we will *not* play. The more alternative
roles youngsters can choose from and practice while young, the better
suited they will be for making choices as adults.

Our culture values the male body as superior to the female body. It is
stronger, bigger, *tougher,* despite the fact that it does not last as many
years. In addition, each ethnic group (and we are all from ethnic groups)
tends to value the physical qualities of their own clan above those of
other clans. But this becomes confused by cultural norms depicted in the
media which emphasize the superiority of white male Caucasian characteristics.

SECURE/INSECURE

If somehow you have managed to be fairly secure about your body,
you will, first of all, respect your own body. You will not be inclined to
destroy it, either through the use of drugs or other insane practices (driving 100 mph). You will be able to present your body for what it is worth
without embarrassment or guilt. You will be free to try out new situations and not be afraid to fail or make a fool of yourself. You will com-
fortably accept your own sex with no need to distort, exaggerate, or hide
your sexuality. (Some men develop large muscles through weight training and the use of steroids in order to feel *macho.* Similarly, some women
show off their bodies, sometimes to the extent of working as topless
dancers or having silicone injections, in order to feel like women.) If you
are secure, you will understand your assets and liabilities realistically
and be comfortable with limitations you don't care to change. If, on the
other hand, you have insecurities, you may be lacking one or more of
the above capabilities (Hunt, 1958).

RESEARCH — PHANTOM LIMB

Research on people who lose limbs through accidents indicates that
most of them suffer what is called a *phantom limb,* an ability to feel the
missing limb, often painfully or pricklingly, even though the limb is not
there to feel. Sometimes this condition can result in a psychotic condition where all of the individual's attention is directed toward the missing
arm or leg. Studies on youngsters before the age of seven indicate that

when they lose a limb they do not experience this condition. The conclusion is that we do not have a fully developed body concept until the age of seven, because after age seven we quite severely miss a body part when it is gone. (This may also be related to myalinization of the neurons and perhaps to Piaget's theory relating to concrete operations.)

HIGH BARRIER SCORES

Fisher and Cleveland (1958) developed a method for using the Rorschach Test to give responses oriented to body surfaces which result in a *Barrier Score*. The method is derived from a subject's response to what he sees in various parts of each ink blot and is based on content involving distinctive surfaces, enclosed openings, or container-like properties. The Barrier Score infers the degree to which people "experience their body boundaries as definite and firm versus indefinite and vague." High Barrier scores (implying thick well-defined surface) show a high positive correlation with exterior body symptoms (arthritis, dermatitis, exterior body cancer). Low Barrier scores (implying thin, easily-permeated surface) show a high positive correlation with interior symptoms and reactivity (colitis, stomach disturbance, and interior body cancer).

FIELD DEPENDENCE/INDEPENDENCE

In separate studies during the 1950s, Witkin et al. and Werner et al. attempted to discover whether people were field-dependent (that is, relying on sensory information other than kinesthesia) or field-independent (relying on kinesthesia primarily). They used several tests. One involved taking the subject into a dark room and seating him in a level chair and asking him to align a neon rod in a neon frame at the other end of the room to a true vertical or a true horizontal. (The gear controlling the rod was next to the subject's chair.) On this test, men and women performed equally well. The next test involved seating the subject in a tilted chair in a dark room. Again, subjects were asked to line up the neon rod. Men performed significantly better than women. Next, subjects took the *Embedded Figure Test* which involved finding a particular figure in an ambiguous field. Again, men did significantly better than women. Success on these tests was termed *field-independence* and was believed to indicate an ability to use one's kinesthetic senses to a greater extent than those who did poorly (called *field-dependent*).

We suggest that perhaps split-brain research offers a different clue. Since men see details (and are more left-brained) while women see wholes (and are more right-brained), detailing abilities may be more important in the male upbringing than in female upbringing. Certainly this hypothesis seems reasonable when considered in conjunction with the Embedded Figure Test.

BODY CONCEPT/SELF CONCEPT

Zion (1963) studied college freshmen women to determine if there was a correlation between the extent to which one valued one's body and the extent to which one valued one's self (intellectual, social, and emotional qualities). She developed a body attitudes survey consisting of fifteen different Guttman (unidimensional) scales of body valuing. She found high positive correlations between scores on these scales on Bill's Index of Adjustment and Values (a self concept scale). It was her conclusion that this was a fertile field for further study of the basic development, interactions and inseparableness of body/self because the relationships between body concept and self concept were so significant.

CONCLUSION

As we interact with our culture, we learn such things as: how attractive or unattractive we are; how large or small we are; how strong or weak we are; how nearly we achieve masculine or feminine standards; how much worth we have; how capable or incapable we are and in what ways. The decisions we arrive at in regard to these value-laden physical qualities have considerable bearing on how we dress, move, touch, groom, exercise, diet, tranquilize, drug, excite, camouflage, despair of and enjoy ourselves, choose careers, choose risks, etc. (Fisher, 1973).

ACTIVITIES

1. Draw and Trace Your Body

A. Get two pieces of butcher paper at least as long and as wide as your body.

B. Draw yourself as you imagine yourself to be on one piece of paper. Look it over carefully. Be as accurate as possible.

C. Have your partner trace an outline of your body on the second sheet of paper while you lie down on it on a hard surface. (Colored chalk usually works well.)

D. Compare the drawing and the tracing and note their similarities and differences.

E. Fill in both pictures and tape them up in your home where you will see them often. Become aware of the good things you see in them.

2. This Is My Nose

A. With at least one other person, you be the leader and say, "This is my nose," (while one hand holds your knee). The other person asks, "Your what?" You say "My nose." Then the other person must correctly reverse the verbal statement with the hand indicator so he will say, "This is my knee," (while one hand holds his nose). Then you say, "Your what?" and he says, "My knee." Continue to verbalize one part of the body while physically indicating a different part with this same kind of interchange.

B. Speed up the procedure to make it more challenging.

3. Mirroring

A. Put some rhythmical music on and have your partner stand in front of you. He is supposed to mirror exactly what you do. This is not really supposed to be dancing so keep the foot work to a minimum but use plenty of arm work. When the tune is about half over trade so that your partner is the leader and you are the mirrorer.

CHAPTER X

THE ORGANIZATION OF PHENOMENA

INTRODUCTION

AS WE GROW and interact with the environment we must develop more and more complex thinking functions rather than merely summating quantitative learnings. Methods of coping and the ways in which we organize words change qualitatively as we continue to reconstruct reality. It is the *organization* that we make of data that is important, not just the gathering of data. In this sense, there is no such thing as *mere* data gathering, however, many of us teach as though it were this simple.

KEPHART'S SCHEMA

Kephart (1971) believes we develop through the following stages: (a) motor, (b) motor-perceptual, (c) perceptualmotor, (d) perceptual, (e) perceptual-conceptual, (f) conceptual, and (g) conceptual-perceptual. We start with random movement, progress to hand/eye and then eye/hand, and then we are able to operate with percepts alone. Finally, percepts give way to concepts and eventually, what we think affects what we perceive.

BARSCH'S SCHEMA

Barsch (1968) likes to use the following equation:

$$\frac{\text{CAPABILITY}}{\text{DEMAND}} = \text{MOVEMENT EFFICIENCY}$$

As we meet greater demands, our capability increases, which causes us to seek greater demands. An elementary youngster might read one to three books per year. A high school youngster might read five to ten books per year. A college student might read twenty to thirty books per year. A doctoral candidate will probably read twenty to thirty books per week during peak performance. After completing the doctorate, the same individual will usually return to twenty to thirty books per year because demand is different. (When third and fourth graders can't read, it's because they could not read in first or second grades. The demand was not great enough for the lack of reading ability to show.)

RAKER'S FREELANCE, PATTERN BOUND, AND OPTION SELECTOR

Raker (1969) believes that as the individual experiences, responds, incorporates, and adapts, changes in the organization of phenomena take place. Initially the individual is a freelancer who can contend with only one bit of information at a time. "The world is constant and I am constant. The one bit is an item which cannot be assimilated to internal organization. I make no accommodation. That one bit of information does not require a changing of relationships."

When a small person is first playing basketball, he is usually primarily concerned with the one bit, "make baskets." Beginners are all shooting every time they get the ball whether they have the strength and skill to make baskets or not, whether they have five opponents guarding them or not.

Later they become pattern-bound. They have a schema, a social convention used to organize the world, but they do not learn the world as it is when organized by that social convention. In basketball they continue to do a *fake and go* whether their guard stays with them or not, or they continue to use a zone defense even when the zone is continually overloaded.

Finally, if all concerned are very lucky and very well taught, they learn to be option-selectors. The social convention becomes a part of their assimilations and they move in a new world with new information. A world of entities and items is traded for a world of relationships. It is a basically different, not a basically similar reality. When such individuals play basketball they are aware of the relationships among the five opponents, the four teammates and themselves from second to second as the space/time of the game changes. They are also aware of the options that are available as these interrelationships change.

MAPS OF THE UNIVERSE

We all create "maps" in our heads of the reality we can construct from our experiencing of the *out there — in here*. Sometimes these maps are effective (knowing how to get home, do square roots, construct a sentence, bake a pie, set a carburetor, etc.) and like a road map will lead to a specific place. Some maps, however, are highly ineffective and lead to difficulties, such as those of the schizophrenic. Other maps are simply barren, such as my own map of astrophysics, which I simply avoid using. (When I have the need, I hire an astrophysicist, a lawyer or an engineer.) However, not everyone has the choice to invoke or hire an effective map, paticularly if the ability is related to the three R's or to learning how to learn or think.

AGNEW AND PYKE

The maps of Agnew and Pyke (1978) involve a somewhat different terminology. They use the word *pragmatic* for the idiosyncratic phase of learning (corresponding to Raker's freelance and Piaget's sensorimotor and preoperational) when all of our meanings and constructions are uniquely our own. They use the word *semantic* for the phase when we learn how to use language to express our thoughts and communicate with others. This phase (corresponding to Raker's pattern-found and Piaget's concrete operational) is grammatical and starts to take over after the youngster is in school and finds it necessary to communicate with others in a language other than his own. Finally they use the term *syntactic* for the time when we become aware of the rules that govern the rules that govern language, or the rules that govern the rules that govern politics, education, or mathematics, etc. (The syntactic phase corresponds with Raker's option selector and Piaget's formal operations.)

PIAGET

As mentioned in Chapter II, Piaget believes that we move through four distinctive patterns of development that occur chronologically. Some people never reach the final formal operations period. Swiss students do much better in achieving Piaget's goals than do American students. (Of course, most of the Swiss schools teach toward Piaget's goals which is rarely true in the United States.)

Most of us who teach are especially concerned with teaching *content*. Raker, Agnew and Pyke, and Piaget would have us teach *process* instead. One can "learn to learn" in a number of ways.

ACTIVITIES

1. Wearing a blindfold, sit on the floor where there is free space within a five foot radius. Get a sense of where you are and make a map of all the space there is in this room. Your partner will then throw a bean bag to various locations. You are to point to that location every time you hear it land. One throw will be directly in front of you and one throw will be directly behind you. The others should be thrown randomly. Think about your first map of this space. Has it changed any as a result of this auditory invasion of your space?

2. Make a target on some newsprint or typing paper and tape it to the wall about shoulder height. With a bean bag or softball, practice throwing underhand from about ten feet away from the target. Then put on the blindfold and make 10 throws. Your partner will retrieve the ball (or bag) and advise whether you were high or low, right or left of the target. You should be able to direct the ball or bag by changing the way in which your fingers contact it as it leaves your hand. Now think about how you have changed your throwing strategies and techniques. Has this changed your map of yourself and the space around you?

3. Hand Mirroring. Two people face one another. One leads and the other follows. The leader moves his hands in any pattern while the follower keeps up so that he is in the same relative space/time. Speed up movements and see how well the follower can keep up. Switch roles. Is there a difference in your feelings when you think the leader is trying to move too fast for your abilities?

4. Body Mirroring. This is an extension of hand mirroring and involves using the whole body, not just the hands. With a partner, one leads and one follows. The leader may use the feet to step forward or backward or sideward. She may use head and face movements as well as

arm, hand, and torso movements. This is usually more difficult than hand mirroring. Reverse roles. Did you find that some movements were easier than others? Did you find that you could predict the movements of your partner? How does she "give herself away?"

5. Knee Tag. There are no leaders or followers, but you will need someone to play with. The object of the game is to tag the opponent's knees while keeping him from tagging your knees. The winner must tag his opponent's knees five times while keeping his opponent from tagging his knees the same number of times. Notice we didn't refer to *partner* this time, but we did use the word *opponent*. Knee tag is a competitive game; one related to mastery of the body, especially directionality and space/time abilities.

CHAPTER XI

DIAGNOSIS AND INDIVIDUALIZED PROGRAMS

THERE ARE several tests available that attempt to measure various perceptualmotor qualities of individuals. Many are primarily designed to be used by researchers who need reliable statistical measures with which to compare different treatment groups. Some are designed for classroom use so that teachers can better understand the needs of each student. These two different groups necessarily produce very different tests.

One researcher was greatly upset when he used Kephart's Purdue Perceptualmotor Survey as a research tool. He found that it was not amenable to statistical treatment and blamed Kephart (who created the survey for *individual diagnosis*) instead of himself for not investigating the purpose of the test in the first place.

THE LINCOLN-OSERETSKY

The Lincoln-Oseretsky is a more effective research tool than educational tool. It is administered individually and consists of thirty-six items incorporating a wide variety of motor skills including finger dexterity, eye-hand coordination, and gross limb and trunk skill. It is more a motor skills test than a perceptualmotor skills test, but has often been used to evaluate perceptualmotor programs. It takes about one to one and one-half hours to administer to a single student.

FROSTIG

The Frostig movement skills test battery consists of twelve items which test gross and fine coordination, muscle strength, balance, and dexterity. It is administered individually and takes twenty to twenty-five minutes per child. It is designed to evaluate youngsters six to twelve years of age. It is more a diagnostic tool than a research tool (Frostig and Maslow, 1973).

AYRES

The Southern California Perceptualmotor Tests developed by A. Jean Ayres (1973) includes six items that are individually administered. They include imitation of postures, crossing mid-line of body, bilateral motor coordination, right-left coordination, standing balance with eyes open, and standing balance with eyes closed. While this test is a research tool, it could be adapted for classroom use.

SMITH

The Perceptualmotor Test development by Paul Smith (1973) is individually administered (in about fifteen minutes) and consists of eleven items including posture, balance, flexibility, awareness of up-down, laterality-bilaterality, unilaterality, cross laterality, hand preference, eye preference, fist preference, and eye control. It was designed to predict potential learning problems of children entering the first grade and so is limited to students at this level.

PURDUE PERCEPTUALMOTOR SURVEY

The Purdue Perceptualmotor Survey was developed by Eugene Roach and Newell Kephart (1966) to provide teachers with a tool for identifying those children who do not possess the perceptualmotor abilities necessary for acquiring academic skills by ordinary instructional methods. It is not a research tool (although researchers continue to criticize it because it isn't). It is administered individually and includes the following eleven items: walking board, jumping, identification of body parts, imitation of movements, obstacle course, Kraus-Webber, Angels In the Snow, chalkboard rhythmic writing, ocular pursuits, and visual achievement forms. We found this a good perceptualmotor testing device for classroom teachers, but we also found it difficult for evaluators to make a transition from test score results to what to do about the youngster. So we created the following test.

THE ZISC

The ZISC originally contained fifteen items, including many items from Kephart's Purdue Perceptualmotor Survey, some from Barsch, some from Cratty, and some from Zion. This was used in several elementary schools in Arcata and Eureka, California. It was found to be useful and needed. After three years' use in its original form, a Humboldt State University student, Dennis Schollard, volunteered to make the directions for each subtest more direct and clear. The original test compiler, Zion, was inspired to evaluate test items and reduce them from fifteen to the present number, ten. As a result, the ZISC (ZI from Zion and SC from Schollard) was created. Interestingly, most of the items from the Purdue Perceptualmotor Survey were retained.

The main purpose of this test is to assist evaluators as they make a transition from identifying perceptualmotor qualities to identifying ways in which to deal with each student. (Descriptions of developmental activities help in making this transition and are described at the end of this chapter.)

Using ZISC takes practice, as do all tests. Five to ten practice sessions with different youngsters are desirable. ZISC can be administered quickly and efficiently to groups using five different testing stations and five qualified test administrators. Administered individually, ZISC takes thirteen to thirty minutes per person.

The key to using ZISC is to complete the Diagnostic Integration Sheet. Once all ten of the subtests have been completed, the items checked can be transposed onto the Diagnostic Integration Sheet by tallying one mark opposite each letter indicated. If you had checked the third and fourth items in No. 1 Walking, you would then put a tally opposite A; a tally opposite B; a tally opposite D; a tally opposite F; a tally opposite J; and a tally opposite K; and so on.

Once the user has determined the strengths and weaknesses of each student (greater number of tallies = weakness), the next step is to consult the Developmental Sequence of PMD Activities and choose activities from those areas to build strengths.

THE ZISC PERCEPTUALMOTOR SCREENING DEVICE

EQUIPMENT: Walking board or an 8 foot 2x4 board; basketball; jump rope; mat; chalkboard; chalk erasers; tests; pencils.

INTRODUCTION

The classroom pupil of today must have a strong foundation of perceptualmotor experiences and abilities in order to meet the rigorous demands of his environment. Each child on entering the educational setting is assumed to have reached the psychophysiological maturation of a five or six year old. It is upon this base of perceptualmotor capabilities that each teacher in succeeding years will build the necessary intellectual progression. Such basic classroom subjects as math and reading require that the child be able to focus attention on specific abstract ideas, connect these items to previous concrete experiences, thereby achieving understanding.

The child with deficits in the perceptualmotor areas will often have problems organizing information into a coherent unit. Ofttimes performance is erratic in nature. In one task concerning balance the child may show great success while in a slightly varied task she will fail. The confusion and frustration experienced by both student and teacher is apparent.

It is the purpose of this screening device to pinpoint those areas in which the child is experiencing perceptualmotor difficulties. Since these difficulties sometimes appear in an erratic manner, a sequence of ten tests is provided to assess the child's capabilities under varied circumstances and to assure an accurate evaluation.

Our thanks to Newell Kephart, Bryant Cratty, and Ray Barsch for introducing us to most of these test items.

DIRECTIONS

Prior to administering the test the examiner should familiarize himself with the format of administration and scoring. Below each test instruction are the possible symptoms which, if exhibited by the child, indicate a problem in one of the main areas of her perceptualmotor abilities. This list of symptomatic criteria corresponds to the Diagnostic Integration Sheet on the back page.

Administering the screening device consists of (1) following the instructions given for each test, (2) marking the symptoms noted, and (3) tabulating the marks on the Diagnostic Integration Sheet at the end.

Example: Test 1

Walking: Position the child so that she is facing you

(M) Toes point out <u>x</u>

(A,B) One leg shows longer stride than other <u>x</u>

In the first instance the child demonstrated a tendency to point her toes outward when walking. The screener marked the space next to the symptom. Later, upon completion of all the tests, the symptomatic criteria would be tabulated using the letter to the left of the symptom description. In this example (M) would be marked once, since toeing indicates a possible problem with pronated ankles.

During administration of the test if the child exhibits an inability to begin a task, further elaboration of the verbal instructions should be given by the examiner. In case the child still cannot begin the task, the teacher may then demonstrate the task. Finally, should the above prove unsuccessful, the examiner should guide the child through the task to a point where he could complete it unassisted if possible. Comments should be noted beside the scoring sheet if *any elaboration* of the instructions was required.

1. *Walking.* Position the child so that he is approximately 30 feet away and facing the screener. Instruct, "Walk toward me." When he has come about 20 feet say, "Now stop. Turn around and face the place where you started and walk back."

(A, B)	One leg shows longer stride than other. _____
(J)	Arms do not coordinate with legs; right arm moving forward when left foot moves forward, etc. _____
(A, B)	Predominant use of one side; right or left side leads. _____
(D, F, J, K)	Trunk of body shows rigidity. _____
(A, B, K)	Arms move very rigidly. _____
(M)	Pronated ankles, improper downward turning of ankles. _____

Comments:

2. *Identification of Body Parts.* Tests the child's body image, awareness of body parts and their interrelationships. The child is to stand facing you. Instruct, "I'm going to ask you to touch parts of your body. As you touch them I want you to also name them." When naming pairs of body parts say, "Touch your hands," etc. Continue with head, toes, back, ankles, shoulders, waist, wrists, knees and elbows.

  (G)   Inability to name one or more parts. _____
  (G)   Inability to name many parts. _____
  (G)   Hand placement somewhat off target. _____
  (G)   Trouble concentrating. _____
  (G)   Must verbalize prior to imitation. _____
  (G)   Shows considerable hesitation. _____
  Comments:

3. *Walking Board.* The child is asked to walk forward, backward, and sideways along the wide edge of a 2x4 board. Situate the child on the floor at one end of the board. Instruct, "Get up on the board and walk to the other end." Next, ask the child to return to the starting point. Now, holding your hand high, at arm's reach say, "I want you to walk across the board again, but this time look at my hand." When he has come to the far end of the board, say, "Now walk backward." When he has returned to the starting point instruct, "Now walk it sideways." Upon completion of walking sideways in one direction instruct, "Once again walk sideways back to the starting point." Make sure he's facing in the same direction in order that his opposite foot will lead this time.

  (D, F, H, J) Upper or whole trunk shows rigidity. _____
  (D, H, J)   Child exhibits jerky movements. _____
  (A, B, D)   Child consistently falls or leans to the right. _____
  (A, B, D)   Child consistently falls or leans to the left. _____
  (A, B, H)   Rigidity of the arms. _____
  (F, G)   One side of the body higher than other. _____
  (A, B, J)   Right leg uncoordinated. _____
  (A, B, J)   Left leg uncoordinated. _____

(D, H, J, K)   Child cannot perform task accurately at a slow pace. _____

(D, E)   Poor performance exhibited when looking at teacher's hand. _____

(D, G)   Occasional difficulty in maintaining balance. _____

(D, G)   Pauses frequently during performance. _____

(D, E, G)   Cannot perform task backwards without looking. _____

(A, B)   Sideways performance considerably better in one direction than in other. _____

Comments:

4. *Jumping and Hopping.* The child's ability to establish and maintain motor rhythm patterns is observed, as well as motor flexibility and the ability to shift control from one side of the body to the other. Situate the child in an area free of obstacles, then instruct (1) "Using both feet jump forward twice, then backward twice." (2) "Now using your right foot only, hop forward once; now do it using only your left foot." (3) "While staying in one place I want you to hop once on the right foot, then once on the left foot, once on the right foot, then once on the left foot, etc." If the child stops after each hop, ask her to go faster. (4) "Again staying in one place I want you to hop twice with the left foot, then once with your right foot. Do this several times." (5) "Now hop once with the left foot and twice with your right foot. Do this several times."

(A, B, G)   Cannot hop on the right foot. _____

(A, B, G)   Cannot hop on the left foot. _____

(A, B, C, D)   Cannot alternate hops. _____

(B, C, D)   Cannot maintain a regular rhythm. _____

(B, C, D)   Cannot maintain an irregular rhythm. _____

(A, B, D, F, G) Cannot jump forward and balance, keeping both sides of the body parallel. _____

(B, C, D, G)   Considerable difficulty in alternate hops. _____

Comments:

5. *Rolling the ball.* The child will need to be situated in a crouching position approximately 10 feet in front of you. Instruct, "I'm going to roll the ball to you and I want you to stop it, and then roll it back to me." First roll it toward the center. Then vary it, rolling to the child's right and then to his left. Next, position the child so that he is again standing about 10 feet in front of you. Instruct, "I'm going to bounce the ball to you. I want you to catch it and bounce it back to me." Make sure you bounce it at an easy height for him to catch.

(E, G)	Does not look at the ball when catching. _____
(A, B, E)	Difficulty with roll on the right. _____
(A, B, E)	Difficulty with roll on the left. _____
(A, B, E)	Difficulty with bounce on the right. _____
(A, B, E)	Difficulty with bounce on the left. _____
(B, E)	Difficulty with roll in the center. _____
(B, E)	Difficulty with bounce in the center. _____

Comments:

6. *Jump Rope.* Provide the child with a jump rope and position her in an open area providing enough room for the activity. Then say, "I want you to jump rope in the way you find most comfortable." Then, "Now try jumping a different way." If she was jumping with both feet ask her to lead with the left foot. Once again ask her to change her method of jumping, this time possibly leading with the right foot. Additional verbal instructions or a demonstration may be necessary. Upon completion of the above tasks tell her, "I want you to jump rope in the way you find easiest. However, this time spell your name backwards when you jump, one letter for each jump." Note in all cases, look for which side, system or part breaks down first.

(A, B, J, G)	Cannot jump rope. _____
(A, B, J, G)	Can only jump backwards. _____
(M)	Flat feet. _____
(C, F, G)	Can turn rope with arms but jumps at the wrong time. _____
(A, B, J)	One arm turns rope; the other arm does very little. _____

(A, B, C, G)   Can only jump rope with one style. _____

(B, C, G)   Cannot spell name backwards and jump at the same time. _____

Comments:

7. *Angels In the Snow*. Determines the child's coordination of body parts and general body image. Position the child so that he is lying on his back on the floor, with arms at his side and feet together. Allow enough room so that the child may freely extend his arms and legs. Before proceeding on to the required task give the child a brief demonstration. Initially ask him to fully extend his arms out along the floor, arching upward, till they are above his head. The hands should be able to touch. Then ask him to move his feet wide apart; his heels should remain on the floor. When this is complete, tell the child, "Move just this arm." The examiner should then point to the appropriate arm. In the first case, it is the right. "Now move your arm back to your side." Each of the following body parts are pointed to in the above manner: (1) right arm, (2) left arm, (3) right leg, (4) left leg, (5) both arms, (6) both legs, (7) left arm and left leg, (8) right arm and right leg, (9) right arm and left leg, (10) left arm and right leg. Next instruct the child to close his eyes. This time he is to extend whichever arms or legs are touched. The examiner then runs the child through a slightly varied version of the above exercises.

(A, B, G)   Overflow of left side movements, those not required. _____

(A, B, G)   Overflow of right side movements, those not required. _____

(A, B, G)   Mixes up responses. _____

(A, B, G)   Cannot correct after one wrong repetition. _____

(A, B, G)   Hesitates. _____

(E, G)   Difficulty identifying the proper limb from visual cues. _____

(G)   Difficulty identifying the proper limb from tactual cues. _____

(B, G)   Inability to reproduce movement pattern. _____

Comments:

8. *Imitation of Movements.* Tests the child's ability to interpret visual cues and relate this information back to her body image and control. Situate the child so that she is standing about three or four feet away facing you. Tell her, "I'm going to move my arms. I want you to move your arms just like I do." Allow a short pause in between movements for the child's response.

(E, G)	Mirrors inconsistently. _____
(A, B, E, G)	Moves left with left and right with right but sometimes changes to mirroring. _____
(E, G)	Hesitates. _____
(E, G)	Does recognize errors and corrects them. _____
(G)	Trouble concentrating, poor attention span. _____
(B, G)	Inappropriate dropping or movement of one arm when other arm is moving. _____
(B, E, G)	Does not move appropriate parts. _____

Comments:

9. *Ocular Pursuits.* Determines the child's ocular control and ability to converge on objects. Use a pencil or other object that can easily become a moving target. Instruct, "I want you to look at this object and follow it with your eyes." Move the pencil around in front of the child; be sure to note whether his eyes follow it. Next, using a piece of paper divide the right side of the face from the left side by holding the paper sideways directly in front of the child's face. (The right visual hemisphere should be separated from the left visual hemisphere.) Again, move the pencil on each side of the paper. Watch the child's eyes to see whether the eyes, though separated, move together, in a coordinated manner. Finally put the pencil about 1 1/2 feet in front of the the child; ask him to touch it. Then move the pencil forward till it almost touches his nose. Notice if the eyes begin to cross.

(A, B, E, L)   Both eyes fail to follow the pencil most of the time. _____

(A, B, E, L)   Both eyes fail to follow the pencil some of the time. _____

(A, B, E, L)   Right eye fails to follow the pencil some of the time. _____

(A, B, E, L)   Left eye fails to follow the pencil some of the time. _____

(B, E, G)   Moves head more than eyes. _____

(A, B, G, L)   Eye movements not smooth and well coordinated. _____

(A, B, G, L)   Eye movements slower than target. _____

(A, B, G, L)   Eye movements ahead of target. _____

(N)   Exhibits hesitation when pencil crosses body midline. _____

(L, B)   Inability to hold fixation on target. _____

(L, B)   Failure to converge (cross eyes) evenly or hold convergence. _____

Comments:

This last item should only be used if there is plenty of time.

10. *Chalkboard Exercise.* Determines the child's directionality, laterality, midline problems, visual-motor match, form perception, and rhythm. Put a small cross + on a blackboard. Position the child so that she is facing the blackboard and looking at the cross. Provide her with two pieces of chalk, one for each hand. Say to her, "I'm going to ask you to draw several shapes. I want you to draw two of whatever I mention. One drawing will be done with the left hand, the other with the right. These are both to be done at the same time."

A. "Draw two circles."

B. "Draw two up-and-down vertical lines."

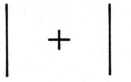

C. "On top of the vertical lines draw two lines that go sideways (horizontal)."

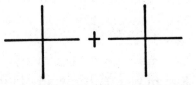

D. "Now I'm going to put two pairs of X's on the board. Again using both hands draw a line between the X's"

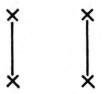

E. "Now draw each of the following numbers twice."

$$
\begin{array}{cc}
1 & 1 \\
2 & 2 \\
3 & 3
\end{array}
$$

F. "With your left hand draw the odd numbers starting with 1. At the same time with your right hand draw the even numbers starting with 2."

$$
\begin{array}{cc}
1 & 2 \\
3 & 4 \\
5 & 6
\end{array}
$$

The following requires that the child only use one hand, whichever he prefers.

G. Draw two X's on the board. Tell the child, "Using one hand draw one line between the X's, going from left to right."

Finally tell the child, "I'm going to draw several things on the board. After I finish each one I want you to copy it on the blackboard." The following should be drawn (handwritten).

H.   *elelelelel*

I.   *pbpbpbpbpb*

J.   *mnmnmnmnmn*

K. On the last drawing start with the large square. Stop. Have the child copy it. Continue on with the rectangle, square, and then add a circle and a triangle. Be sure to stop after drawing each shape.

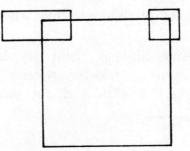

(A, B)	Left hand weak. _____
(A, B)	Right hand weak. _____
(A, B, E, G)	Mirrors figures (draws them backwards). _____
(A, B, G, H)	Figures are small. _____
(A, B, G)	Scribbles. _____
(A, I)	Has difficulty holding chalk. _____
(A, E, G)	Fails to reproduce handwriting samples. _____
(A, B, E, G)	Lopsided circles, X's, lines, connecting lines. _____
(E, G)	Fails to place figures in right place on square. _____

(E, G)	Fails to reproduce geometric shapes accurately. _____
(E, G)	Poor reproductions. _____
(N)	Vertical lines are bowed. _____
(E, G)	Figures and shapes vary widely in size. _____
(E, G)	Figures and shapes are formed inaccurately. _____
(A, B, E, G)	Figures and shapes incorrectly oriented. _____
(N)	Child exhibits difficulty in crossing midline of body with hand. _____
(A, B, G, J)	Incoordination of two hands. _____
(A, B, J)	Considerable hesitation. _____
(A, B, I)	Lack of finger dexterity. _____
(A, B, I)	Lack of wrist dexterity. _____
(B, C, G)	Lack of synchronization between the two arms. _____
(E, G)	Reversal of figures. _____
(C, G)	Lack of rhythmic flow when writing or drawing. _____
(A, B, G)	Right-handed child should draw right circle counter clockwise, reverse for left-handed child. Mark if child did not show this characteristic. _____

Comments:

DIAGNOSTIC INTEGRATION SHEET

ONLY ONE CHECK MARK NECESSARY
TO WARRANT PURSUING PROBLEM:

A. Internal Directionality (internally understanding the separate use of the right and left side of the body) _____

B. External Directionality (ability to use both sides of the body simultaneously) _____

C. Rhythm (ability to move to more than one cadence) _____
D. Balance (ability to distribute weight evenly on each side of the vertical axis) _____
E. Visual-Motor Match (pairing of visual and motor senses) _____
F. Trunk Awareness (ability to distinguish trunk parts) _____
G. Body Awareness (internal awareness of body parts and their interrelationships) _____
H. Relaxation (ability to eliminate tension in the body) _____
I. Strength (ability to exert power when needed) _____
J. Coordination (ability to move various parts of the body harmoniously to bring about a common action) _____
K. Flexibility (ability to adapt to new and changing requirements along with extending the range of movement of various body parts) _____
L. Needs Eye Exam (unable to track a moving object properly) _____
M. Pronated Ankles (improper downward turning of the ankles, usually accompanied by flat feet) _____
N. Midline Problem (hesitates to move hand through midline or center of body, going from right to left or vice versa) _____

DEVELOPMENTAL PERCEPTUALMOTOR ACTIVITIES

A. Body Awareness

1. Lacy Fingers
   Interlace the fingers of both hands. Press the palms together hard. Hold for a count of three, then relax pressure. Repeat 10 times.
2. Head Bends
   Bend the head to one side, keeping the face forward so that maximum tension is felt in the neck muscles of the opposite side. Keep other parts of the body still. Hold for a count of 3; relax and return to the original position. Bend to the other side.
3. Round Backs
   Sit on the floor cross-legged with the hands behind the neck, fingers interlaced. Press the hands against the neck rounding the back, bend forward as far as possible. Press the neck down with the

hands. Hold for a count of 3. Repeat. Lie on the floor to relax.

4. Rocking Chair

   Sit on the floor with the hips and knees bent and feet on the floor. Shift body weight onto the lower back, let the feet rise off the floor. At the same time, bend the head and shoulders forward. Hold to a count of 3. Return to a sitting position without using the hands.

5. Rag Doll

   On a mat, have the children practice falling like a rag doll from a standing position. The children can also fall from a kneeling position. Once they have fallen have them relax in that position for 15-30 seconds.

6. Something Going on Inside

   Have the children lie on their backs with the eyes closed. Have them become aware of the heart rate and breathing.

7. Lazy Knees

   a. Lie on the back, relaxed. Slowly raise the knees, slide feet along the floor toward the buttocks. Relax tension of the leg muscles and slide the feet back to the original position.

   b. As in a, but letting the knees and lower leg fall to the right, touching the floor instead of the feet sliding. Then swing the bent knees with as little effort as possible to the left. Repeat.

8. Lazy Arms

   Lie on the back, relaxed; raise the arms slowly to a vertical position. Relax the muscles and let the arms drop to the floor. Repeat.

9. Loose Galloose

   Relax the arm and leg muscles by shaking them. Stand with the body weight on the one foot, shaking the free leg and arms. May also sit on the floor or lie down and shake the arms and legs.

10. Robots.

    Lie on the back with eyes closed. The teacher names a body part which the child moves gently. You can combine more than one body part if so inclined.

11. Giant's Breath

    Stand in an upright position, holding the arms out horizontally. Droop the head. Breathe in steadily while raising head and lowering the arms. Exhale while drooping the head and raising arms to the original horizontal position.

12. Elf's Breath

    Kneel, sit on the heels, and bend the torso forward in a relaxed position. The head is hanging near the floor. Breathe in steadily while straightening the back with the head raised. Rise to an upright position. Relax to the first position while exhaling. Each child should flow and follow her own breathing rhythm.

13. Frogs
Kneel with hands on the floor below the shoulders. Have the thighs at right angles to the floor. Try to press "holes" into the floor with the hands. Hold for a count of 3. Relax, repeat.

14. Bear Back Rub
Stand with your back 4-6 inches from the wall. Lean backward and press against the wall with the back as hard as possible. While pressing, slide towards the floor with knees bent as if sitting in a chair. Slide up to the original position. Repeat.

15. Turtle Shells
With children in twos, standing back to back; one pushes forward, the other provides enough resistance to slowly push across the room. Reverse partners.

16. Roll and Tumble
Have the child crawl through a tunnel. Also have him roll on the floor. He should become aware of touching the floor with various body parts. Do the rolling and crawling slowly.

17. Obstacle Course
Children can be told to crawl under a table, step over a chair, jump over lines drawn on the floor, go around other children, etc. Once the obstacle course is learned, the children can be timed to promote agility and speed in addition to body awareness. You can also have the children start from the end of the course and go backwards to the beginning.

18. This Is It
Have the children assume different positions, such as being small, tall, middle size, having 1, 2, 3, or 4 points on the ground. Have one child as leader shouting "this is it" as she assumes the position to be mimicked.

19. Right Hand, Left Hand
Separate children into right- and left-hand dominant groups. Have the child hold a beanbag in the dominant hand while slowly raising the dominant arm forward to a horizontal position on a cue of "right" or "left." As the child raises the arm, he is to name that arm as right or left. Change arms.

20. Point to the Point
    The child is given the cue "right arm point right." Next the teacher says, "turn right" and the child makes a quarter-turn to the right without moving the pointing arm, thus ensuring that the finished movement faces in the same direction as the arm is pointing. The left-handed child does it to the left.

21. Clock Hands
    Practice jumping quarter- and half-turns. Play a game in which directions for jumping are given, such as half-turn, quarter-turn-left, quarter-turn-right, etc.

22. Detour Obstacles
    Follow a chalk line until an obstacle is encountered which has been set either to the right or left of the line. The child must point to the obstacle, state whether the obstacle is right or left and proceed to climb over or go under the obstacle.

23. Simon Says
    Sit on the floor, knees bent and feet flat on the floor. Commands, "right hand on left knee," "cross arms in front of chest," "right hand on left eye," etc. are given by the teacher. Children repeat each direction while following the command.

24. Do You Know How?
    The children stand and follow such commands as clap twice, put your elbows together, touch one elbow, put your knees together, touch the right knee with the left hand, touch left knee with right hand, touch your nose with one hand, draw a square in the air, etc.

25. Angels In the Snow.

26. Draw around a partner on butcher paper.

27. Jump and turn by half-turns, and then by whole turns with eyes closed.

28. Broad Jump
    Have each child estimate her distance.

29. Jump and reach (for height).

30. Blind Walk (without shoes).

31. Fitting Through and Into Objects.

32. Partner Stunts
    a. Chest stand
    b. Angel balance
    c. Swan balance
    d. Reverse angel balance

33. Left/Right Judgements
    Pointing one-by-one to body parts, have students learn to orient themselves to the left or right in relation to objects or entities (e.g., "Place your left side on the nearest wall," OR "Put the scarf in your left hand."

34. Line Jumping
    Stand on or near a line. Jump over the line, forward, backward, jump and turn, hop, hop and turn. Balance on one foot and land on two. Land on left or right foot.

35. Step on the Cracks.

36. Hit the Deck (and rolling exercises).

37. Hokey Pokey.

38. Sand Play
    The object is to let the child draw circles with elbows, hands, thumb, feet, nose. Encourage the child to say, "Around and around it goes and wherever it stops nobody knows." This will help develop a rhythmic movement pattern.

39. Roll a ball and have child hit it with designated body parts. Begin with bilateral, then unilateral.

40. Sticky Sticks
    Have children touch head, knees, etc. while at the same time identifying the parts of body that are being touched.

41. Jostling (more commonly known as wrestling).

42. Tumbling Progression
    a. Half top spin
    b. Full top spin
    c. Forward roll
    d. Backward roll
    e. Dive roll
    f. Tripod
    g. Head stand
    h. Hand stand
    i. Cartwheel.

43. Kraus-Webber Movements.

44. Forward and Backward Rolls.

45. Log Roll.

46. Ball Throwing (overhand and underhand).

47. Rope Jumping.

48. Reach across mid-area of body. Lift shoulders separately on each

side. Sitting position.
49. Passing ball around body.
50. Twister
51. Isolations
   Isolate parts of body for movement. Must learn to feel and move various parts separately.
52. Hula Hoops.
53. Dip
   Place crumpled paper on a mat about 12 inches in front of body. Kneel on mat with hands clasped behind back. Bend head and trunk forward; pick up paper with teeth; return to starting position. Increase distance of paper and repeat.
54. Human Rocker.
55. Duck Walk.
   Take a squat position with feet separated and knees apart. Bend elbows and place hands under armpits for wings. Flap wings as steps are taken. Swing leg out to the side and forward as a new step is taken.
56. Inchworm
   Take a front leaning rest position. Keep hands stationary, flex hips, and walk up to the hands. Keep the feet stationary and walk on the hands away from the feet. Keep knees and elbows straight throughout.

B. Balance

1. Static Balance
   Have the child balance with the help of a chair or another child holding the child's hand. Once the child can balance in a static position, then he is ready to do exercises without support.
2. Standing on Tiptoes
   For all exercises, the heels should be raised as far as possible from the floor.
   a. Children stand, raising themselves to tiptoe position; hold for 3-5 seconds and then return to standing position.
   b. As the children rise on the toes, using both hands slowly raise a ball high overhead.
3. Forward Balance
   a. Stand on one foot and bend forward, raising the free leg backward until the trunk and free leg are parallel to the floor. The

arms are held at right angles to the body. Hold this position to the count of 5. Return to a standing position. Repeat with the other leg.

   b. As a, but raise the arms in front.

   c. Try to balance on one leg with the trunk and arms in any position. Have the child bend backward, sideways, or forward, with the arms in any position.

   d. The children create movement sequences by adopting the original balance position, taking a few steps and adopting another position, and finishing with the original position. Repeat the sequence.

4. Sideways Balance

Proceed slowly with this exercise, going step by step and demonstrating each new movement.

   a. Children sit on the floor with legs straight and slightly apart, arms stretched sideways at right angels to the body. The children bend slowly and rhythmically right and left keeping the arms at the same angles and the back straight to the trunk.

   b. As in a, but the children bend right and left as far as possible.

   c. Stand with feet slightly apart, arms at right angles to the body. Keeping the hips as motionless as possible, bend sideways as far as possible, first to one side, then to the other. Repeat 6 times.

5. One-Leg Swing

   a. Balance on one foot and swing the free leg forward and backward twice. Practice on both left and right.

   b. As in a, but swing the free leg to the side and back twice.

   c. Balancing on one foot, swing the free leg forward and center, swing side and center, swing forward and center. Repeat at least 5 times on both sides to develop a rhythm.

   d. As in c, but swing the free leg side and center, back and center, side and center.

6. Stepping Stones

   a. Step from one block to another. Increase the distance between blocks gradually.

   b. Step to the floor between the steps on the blocks and increase speed. Briefly, hold positions on the blocks.

   c. Jump from disc to disc with both feet together.

   d. Jump with one foot only, alternating, in as smooth a rhythm as possible.

   e. Arrange steps in an irregular pattern. Cross a "river" on all fours, without putting a hand or foot in the "water."

7. The Bicycle
   a. Lie face up; raise legs and lower trunk as nearly vertical as possible, weight on the back of the shoulders with the hands supporting the upper body. Make bicycling movements with the legs.
   b. As in a, but move the legs back and forth like scissors. Keep the legs straight.
   c. From the face-up position, slowly raise the legs up and overhead; keep them straight and close together until the feet touch the floor behind the head. Reach a sitting position by swinging the legs quickly back to the floor, raising the head and the back simultaneously.

8. Water Carriers
   a. Walk along various paths; forward, backward, sideways, twisting and turning with a beanbag balanced on the head.
   b. Change speed while walking, either faster or slower.
   c. Find different ways of moving about, such as skipping, running or walking on tiptoes.
   d. Make up different combinations of movements and turns.
   e. As in a-c, except other parts of the body carry the beanbag; i.e., back of neck, crook of arm, shoulders.

9. Giraffe Walk
   Stretch the arms on or over the head and clasp the hands together forming a giraffe's head and neck. Imitate the giraffe's movement by walking on tiptoes with the legs stretched, knees stiff; arms and trunk may sway slightly but must always point upward.

10. Balance Beam
    a. Walk forward and backward on the beam.
    b. Walk sideways; then back across sideways crossing one leg behind the other.
    c. Practice turning.
    d. Skip, hop, or jump along the beam.
    e. Walk two steps forward, make a half-turn, walk two steps sideways, make a half-turn, and walk two steps forward. Repeat, turning in the opposite direction.
    f. Walk with bent knees, alternate small and large steps, stand, squat, sit down, walk on tiptoes, etc.

11. Statues

a. Stand on the floor and adopt a succession of positions, holding each for a few seconds.

b. As in a, but stand on stools, beams, blocks, or low benches.

c. Children imitate pictures of various positions.

d. In pairs, one child adopts positions for his partner to imitate. Reverse partners.

e. Run in a circle to the beating of a drum. When the beating stops, adopt any position, but only one foot may touch the floor and the trunk may not be erect. Hold for a count of 5 and resume the beating.

12. Balance on two feet (or one foot) with or without your eyes closed.

13. Balance on four (three, two, or one) parts of the body.

14. Use body parts and make various bridges high in the air and/or low to the ground. Remove certain body parts (i.e., balancing on left arm and right leg, etc.).

15. Walk the balance beam forward, backward, and sideways; both with and without a blindfold.

16. Place obstacles on balance beam (or 2x4) to step over.

17. Balance in various positions. Put weight on different body parts.

18. Balance on one foot with arms in varying positions.

19. Balance lightweight puff ball or beanbags on different body parts and conduct relays.

20. Do the activity above with blindfolds and use jump ropes taped to the floor to guide children.

21. Arrange children with partners and have them create their own two-person balance stunts.

22. Tumbling stunts such as:
    a. Half- and full-top spins
    b. Duck walk
    c. Crab walk
    d. Tripod
    e. Head stand
    f. Hand stand
    g. Partner stunts: chest stand, angel balance, swan balance.

23. Hop Scotch.

24. Roller Skating.

25. Bongo Boards.

26. Stilts.

C. Coordination

1. Arm Circles
   a. Sit with the arms stretched out to the sides. Keeping the back straight, make backward circular movements with the arms; increase the size of circles.
   b. As in a, but from a standing position.
2. The Bell
   a. Stand with feet apart, arms relaxed at the side. Bend forward, keeping the knees stiff, and touch the floor. Grasp the ankles and pull steadily trying to bend down as far as possible. Return to the original position.
   b. As in a, but in the bent position, children pretend to be big bells, swinging the arms and trunk forward and backward.
   c. As in b, but on the third swing use the upward swing of the arms as impetus for a jump with feet together and legs extended.
3. Head-to-Foot
   Sit on the floor with legs spread and straight. Lean forward, grasp one ankle with both hands pulling the head down toward the leg. Repeat, alternating sides.
4. Ankle-Hold Walk
   Bend forward, keeping the knees straight, grasp the ankles and walk forward. If this proves too difficult, hold the calves first and progress to the ankles.
5. Elephant Walk
   Link the fingers of both hands and bend forward at the waist; allow the arms to swing loosely. Take a heavy step with the right foot, swing the arms to the right. Repeat with the left foot and arms.
6. Leg Stretch
   Lie face up on the floor; raise one leg as high as possible, keeping the knee straight and the other leg on the floor. Lower the raised leg and repeat with the other side leg.
7. Leg Lift
   a. Standing with feet parallel and slightly apart, slowly raise one leg forward as high as possible, then slowly lower it. Repeat with the other leg.
   b. As in a, but raise each leg to the side.
   c. As in b, but raise each leg to the back.
8. Leg Swing
   a. Standing upright, swing one leg back and forward. Repeat with

the other leg.

  b. As in a, but swing each leg to the side.

  c. As in a, but swing the leg in circles.

  d. As in a, but swing each leg far out in front so that students are forced to take forward steps. Continue these "giant" steps across the room.

9. The Draw Bridge

  Lie on the floor face up. Slowly raise the legs keeping them straight, lowering them over the head until the toes touch the floor. Return slowly to the starting position.

10. Rocking Somersaults

  a. Sit on the floor, knees bent, arms around them. Rock backward until the shoulders touch the floor; rock forward until the feet touch the floor.

  b. As in a, but swing the legs all the way backward and over the head, touching the floor with the toes.

  c. As in b, but pull the knees toward the head and roll completely over, finishing in a kneeling position.

11. Ballet Dancer

  a. Crouch and sit back on the heels, back straight with fingers interlaced behind the neck. Without leaning forward, bend the head and upper trunk alternately sideways to the right and left.

  b. As in a, but from an upright kneeling position.

  c. As in b, but with one leg stretched out to the side.

  d. Standing as high as possible on the toes, try walking, turning, twisting, and bending.

12. Windshield Wipers

  a. Sit on the floor with legs straight in front. Place the hands on the hips turning as far as possible to the right without turning the knees inward or bending forward. Repeat to the left, and then alternate in a smooth and continuous motion.

  b. As in a, but with arms stretched above the head.

  c. As in b, but from a standing position.

13. Head Circles

  Sitting cross-legged, rotate the head in as large a circle as possible, first clockwise, and then counter-clockwise. Slow the movements for maximum stretch. The trunk and shoulders should remain still.

14. Through-the-Tunnel and Over-the-Bridge

  a. Children should stand single file, legs apart to form a tunnel.

The front child passes a large ball between his legs to the child behind and the motion continues to the end of the line.

b. Have the children pass the ball backward over their heads. They should stand far enough apart that backward extension is required.

c. Pass the ball through-the-tunnel and over-the-head, alternately.

15. Train Gate

a. Stand with legs apart. Grasping a 30-inch rod at both ends, raise the rod slowly over the head and as far backward as possible. Keep the arms straight and the trunk upright. Bring the rod slowly back to the front. The rod should be held in a horizontal position.

b. As in a, but sitting with the legs straight.

16. The Rocking Chair

a. Sit on the floor, knees close to the chest, arms around knees, head bent forward, feet off the floor. Roll forward and backward.

b. Some children may be able to gain enough momentum to swing up to a standing position by thrusting the arms forward.

17. Back Roll

a. Lie on the floor face up, raise the legs overhead with knees bent. Bring the knees down on either side of the head as close to the floor as possible. Roll backward to a sitting position. Arms are at the side and may push on the floor for added help.

b. As in a, but try to do the exercise without pushing on the floor.

18. Step Through the Ring

a. Stand upright and lace the fingers together, making a ring with the arms. Pull one knee to the chest, keeping the other leg and back straight; the head and neck may be bent forward. Maintain the position to a count of 3.

b. As in a, but step through the ring, first with one leg, then the other.

19. The Cat

Children should assume a crawling position with the hands and knees on the floor and the back horizontal. Round the back like an angry cat by pulling the head toward the trunk. Straighten the neck and let the spine slowly sink to a resting position.

20. The Mermaid

a. Lie on one side. Raise both legs sideways as high as possible, keeping the legs together. Brace with the arms in front of the chest for support. Repeat for the alternate side.

  b. Lie on one side, arms stretched overhead. Raise the legs and upper part of the body as high as possible and rock up and down on the pivot of the hips. Repeat.

21. Hopping
  a. Hop in place.
  b. Hop three consecutive paces with feet together.
  c. Hop three backward.
  d. Hop backward on the left foot, then the right foot.
  e. Hop three steps sideways with feet together.
  f. Hop to different rhythms. Combine previous steps into varied patterns.
  g. Hop with beanbag on head.
  h. Half and full hop spins.

22. Upswing
  Kneel on the floor with the body erect and weight on the balls of feet. Swing arms back behind the body. Swing arms forward vigorously and rock the body weight back over the balls of the feet. Rise to a standing position.

23. Turk Stand.

24. Bells or Clicks
  Cross the right foot in front of the left. Spring from the forward right foot. Raise the left leg sideways and bring right foot up to meet the extended left leg; click the heels together and land on the floor.

25. Seal Slap
  From a prone position with weight supported on straight arms and toes. Push from mat with hands, throw body up and clap hands in air. Quickly drop hands to mat to break fall. Repeat.

26. Human Rocker
  Lie face down on mat. Bend knees, arch the back, and reach back to grasp the feet. Pull hard on the feet to lift the head and shoulders off the mat. Let the body rock forward onto the chest, then back again to the thighs immediately. Rock back and forth.

27. Frog Dance.

28. Crab Walk
  From a squat position, reach back and put both hands flat on the floor without sitting down. Support the weight equally on both arms and legs. Walk face up in this position.

29. Tailor Stand.
30. Coffee-Grinder.
31. Cross the Creek

    Two parallel lines drawn about two feet apart are the "creek." Children line up in single file and follow the leader in jumping or leaping across it. After each youngster has crossed the creek, it is widened by about six inches. Again they follow the leader. When children fail to make it across, they are out of the game. The creek is continually widened until only the winner remains.

32. Beneath the Bar

    A bar is held between two supports. In pairs, children walk beneath this. The bar is gradually lowered (2-3 inches at a time) until it is so low that the children must crawl underneath it. The rule is that they must maintain contact with their partners and may not touch the cross bar as they pass under it.

33. Eye-Hand Coordination
    a. Beanbag throw at a target, into a basket, and to another person. Practice with one eye, both eyes, and blindfolded.
    b. Give each team a balloon. Conduct relays while keeping the balloon in the air.
    c. Same as in b, but each child has his own balloon and it becomes one big race.
    d. Have children stand in a circle with one standing in the center. The middle child hits the balloon into the air and calls out the name of another child to come hit it next.

34. Eye-Foot Coordination
    a. Ball-kicking relays
    b. Dodge ball
    c. Modified soccer

D. Flexibility

1. Collecting Seashells
   a. Walk forward, going into a knee bend with every step. Pick up an imaginary seashell with the hand opposite the forward foot. Children should advance with a steady rhythmic swing, without pausing after picking up each seashell.
   b. Pick up the seashell with the hand on the same side as the forward foot.
   c. At a signal, bend to pick up seashell, then continue skipping. A

smooth and flowing movement is best.
  d. As in c, but have the child pick her own course and rhythm while skipping, running, and walking.
2. Troll's Walk
  a. Walk, raising knees and stamping feet. Trunk is bent forward with arms stiff and fists clenched.
  b. Continue as in a, bending forward, arms swinging freely while walking. Do not stamp hard.
  c. Raise the feet high with the body straight.
3. Pull-Ups
  a. Lie on the floor face up. Raise each leg alternately to a vertical position; keep the legs straight.
  b. Raise each arm alternately keeping the feet flat on the floor.
  c. Raise both legs together; lower the legs. Raise the left arm and left leg together; lower; repeat with the right arm and right leg. Repeat 5 times.
  d. Raise the right arm and left leg; then left arm and right leg. Repeat 5 times.
4. Round-the-World
  Stand in circles of up to 10 children in each and pass a ball quickly from one to another around the circle. If a child drops the ball, everyone shouts "Get it." The ball must be retrieved and the child runs around the circle with the ball. She returns to her spot in the circle and passing the ball resumes. When the teacher shouts "Round the World," the child holding the ball must run around the circle with it.
5. Figure Jumping
  The teacher forms shapes such as circles, squares, triangles, rectangles, and cubes on the floor. Each child is asked to stand next to a specific shape and jump into it with both feet together. If the shapes are familiar to the children, have them call out the name of the shape before jumping.
6. Basic Rope Jumping
  a. Jump forward and backward over a rope lying on the ground, first with both feet at once. Next, start on two feet and land on one foot.
  b. As in a, but the rope is held a few inches above the ground.
  c. Have the children go over or under the rope in any way they choose.
  d. Jump over a rope that is swinging slowly back and forth.

    e. Each child jumps over a short rope that he turns himself.

7. Side-Step and Slide-Step
    a. Walk sideways placing one foot to the side then placing the other beside it. Repeat in the opposite direction.
    b. As in a, but slide the feet along the floor.
    c. Form a square. Slide 2 steps forward leading with the left foot and slide the right foot up to the left. Then slide 2 steps to the side leading with the right foot, bringing the left foot up to it. Next two slides backward, leading with the right foot, and finish with 2 slides to the left. Practice to both left and right.

8. Cross-Over Walk
    a. Walk sideways in a straight line, placing the left foot to the side and crossing the right foot in front. Return in the other direction, crossing the left foot in front of the right.
    b. As in a, but cross one foot behind the other.
    c. Cross in front and back alternately. Remain facing the teacher without turning the trunk.
    d. As in c, but in pairs facing each other and holding hands.

9. Crawling
    a. Begin on the hands and knees, hands below shoulders, knees under the hips. Move one arm and the opposite leg forward simultaneously. Move the head toward the shoulder of the arm that is *not* extended. Continue, using the opposite arm and leg.
    b. Crawl backward after mastering a, above.
    c. Crawl in patterns and directions. Call out geometric shapes and figures for children to trace.

10. Crab Walk
Squat, and then reach backward, placing hands flat on the floor behind the hips without sitting down. Raise the pelvis as high as possible and move backward and then forward in this position. Keep the head, neck, and trunk parallel to the floor.

11. Magpie, Hop Quickly to Your Nest
    a. Practice a bird hop with feet together, moving forward.
    b. Hop forward as fast as possible. Conduct races.
    c. Hop forward, holding a beanbag between the knees.
    d. Place a beanbag between the feet *without* using the hands. Hop to a goal and then back to the starting point.

12. Galloping
    a. Gallop in a circle.

    b. Change direction at the beat of a percussion instrument.

    c. Moving as individuals, have children alternate galloping, trotting, walking, and running at their own pace and time.

13. Bump-Your-Knee and Touch-Your-Heel

    a. Skip around the room.

    b. While skipping, reach backward and touch the foot of the raised leg with the hand on the same side.

    c. Have children invent their own variations.

14. Catching Beanbags

    a. Each child throws a beanbag into the air and catches it.

    b. Throw beanbag into the air and clap the hands before catching the bag as it comes down.

    c. Throw the beanbag into the air and jump before catching it.

    d. As in c, but land with one leg in front, the other behind. Switch position of legs with each jump.

15. Catching Moving Beanbags

    a. Walk while throwing beanbags in the air and catching them.

    b. As in a, but while running.

16. Catching the Beanbags

    a. Throw a beanbag to a partner about 5 feet away.

    b. Increase the distance between partners gradually.

    c. Stand in pairs close to a box (square drawn on ground, or target). Try to throw the beanbags into the box.

    d. Increase the distance from the box (target).

    e. Have a succession of boxes in which to throw a beanbag. Each child throws her beanbag into the box, retrieves it, and proceeds to the next box (target).

17. Ball Game

    a. Have the children experiment freely by bouncing, catching or throwing balls individually with or without partners.

    b. Pair children up facing each other and bouncing the ball once to get it to the partner.

18. Spikes in a Wheel

    a. Children sit on the floor in 8-10 foot diameter circles, with 6 children to a circle. Each child stretches his legs out to form a "V." One child sits in the center.

    b. The child in the center rolls or bounces the ball to someone in the circle who returns the ball by rolling or bouncing it back. When every child has returned the ball to the center, a new child

takes the center position.
c. Increase the pace, or bounce the ball twice.
19. Hot Potato
   a. Stand in a circle; every third child has a tennis ball. Each ball represents a "hot potato" which will burn if kept in the hand too long. Each child with a ball throws it immediately to any child with empty hands.
   b. If a child drops the ball or throws it erratically, she must take the now "cold potato" to the oven, a designated area where she must throw the ball up and catch it 10 times before rejoining the group.

E. Strength

1. Feathering (leg muscles)
   The child stands 2 feet from a wall while touching the wall with extended and parallel-to-the-floor arms. Move the ankles so that the feet and toes point toward the shins. Stand on tiptoes.
2. Elevator (thigh muscles)
   Adopt an upright kneeling position, keep thighs vertical, and back straight. Slowly sit down on the calves, keeping the back straight and then rise to the upright position. Repeat. (Children experiencing difficulty should perform this exercise with a partner holding the hands.)
3. Shoulder Stand (abdominal muscles)
   Lie on the back on the floor; raise the legs (knees bent), pelvis, and lower trunk from the floor until the weight is resting on the shoulders, neck, and back of the upper arms. Hold the waist with the hands.
4. Leg Piston (leg and abdominal muscles)
   a. Lie on the back and move the legs by bringing one knee back toward the chest as the other is held straight out and on the floor. Bring the raised knee as close to the chest as possible.
   b. As in a, but after returning the bent leg from the chest to the floor, hold it off the floor to a count of 3.
5. Raising Leg Sideways (thigh, trunk muscles)
   a. Lie on the side with the arm closest to the floor straight over the shoulder; rest the head on the extended arm. The opposite arm bends in front of the chest with the hand, palm down on the floor. Slowly raise and lower the top leg. Change sides.

b. As in a, but rotate the raised leg in a circular motion.

6. Look at Me (back muscles)

   Lie face down with hands clasped behind the neck. Slowly raise the head and chest as high as possible. Lower slowly. If there is difficulty keeping the lower trunk and legs on the floor, have a partner hold the ankles.

7. Legs Up (lower back and abdominal muscles)

   Lie face down with arms outstretched to the sides. Raise the legs and lower trunk as high as possible. If there is difficulty keeping the chest down, have a partner hold the shoulders down.

8. Rocking Horse (back, neck, and shoulder muscles)

   Lie face down with arms outstretched to the sides or overhead. Raise the arms, neck, head and legs as high as possible. Rock back and forth in this position.

9. Making a Right Angle (abdominal muscles)

   Lie face up. Raise the legs slowly until they are vertical; lower them slowly. Keep the legs straight with the head and shoulders flat on the floor. It may be necessary to start with one leg in order to get both off the floor in the parallel position.

10. Sit-Ups (abdominal muscles)

    Lie face up with arms to the sides, knees bent. Sit up without using the hands; lean forward and try to touch the toes. Repeat 3-5 times. A partner can hold the ankles if necessary.

11. Bobbing for Apples (arm and shoulder muscles)

    Kneel, hands on the floor with arms straight, back parallel to the floor. Bend arms until the chest is on the floor; allow the feet to rise. Hold this position to a count of 3 before returning to the kneeling position.

12. Sit-Ups with Bent Knees (abdominal muscles)

    Lie face up, arms to the sides with knees bent. Sit up without using the hands; clasp arms around the knees curling up tightly while touching the head to the knees. Repeat 5 times.

13. Circus Seal Walk (shoulder girdle, arm, and back muscles)

    a. Lie face down placing the hands next to the shoulders; straighten the arms in order to raise the upper body. Move forward, walking on the hands and dragging the legs. Keep the legs straight and together.

    b. As in a, but carry a beanbag on the head.

    c. Have the children make up their own "tricks" such as a seal might, i.e., turn on side, roll over, etc.

14. Inchworm (arm, back, and abdominal muscles)
    Lie face down with hands near the shoulders, and balls of the feet on the floor. Straighten the arms, raising the trunk until it is approximately parallel to the floor. Support weight on hands and feet. Keeping the knees straight, walk forward with small steps until the feet are near the hands. Move the hands forward step by step until the trunk is again parallel to the floor. Repeat slowly.

15. Karate Kick (leg and abdominal muscles)
    Lie face up and slowly raise the legs up and over the head until they are parallel to the floor. Support the hips with the hands. Return to a sitting position by swinging the legs down in a rapid motion; raise the head and back simultaneously. Try to avoid helping with the hands. Repeat.

16. Push-Ups (from the bent-knee position for girls).

17. Sit-Ups (bent knee, hands behind head).

18. Reverse Sit-Up (child raises trunk while on stomach).

19. Calisthenics.

20. Tug-O-War.

21. Leg Lifts.

22. Strengthening shoulder girdle and trunk muscles
    a. Sit on floor, knees pulled close to body with feet flat. Lean back, place hands behind to the sides. Children should raise themselves on hands and feet by pushing the trunk upward and parallel to the floor.
    b. Perform rolls from the raised position.

23. Rocking Horse (strengthening back, neck, and shoulder muscles)
    Lie face down, arms outstretched to sides or overhead. Raise arms, neck, head, legs as high as possible from floor.

24. Drawbridge (strengthening abdominal muscles)
    Lie on floor, face up; slowly raise legs, keeping them straight, and then lower the legs overhead until the toes touch the ground.

25. Strengthening Arm Muscles
    Lie face down on floor, hands beside shoulders with palms on floor and elbows bent. Have students stand up by pushing on floor with hands and jumping up.

26. Tailor Stand
    Sit on floor in cross-legged position with arms folded in front of chest, elbows held high. At a signal each yuoungster tries to raise to

a standing position without unfolding his arms or changing his cross-legged position. If he succeeds, he tries to resume a sitting position.

27. Coffee-Grinder

    Each child places his right hand on the floor, keeping arm stiff. He extends both legs out to the left, and keeping the body as straight as possible, walks around in a circle, using the right arm as a pivot.

28. Turk Stand

    Stand with arms and legs crossed, weight on outer edges of feet. Keep legs and arms crossed and sit down easily. Shift weight over feet and rise to standing position. Keep balance to finish as in starting position, arms and legs still crossed.

29. Knee Dip

    Stand with left side to mat. Grasp left ankle behind back with right hand. Bend the right knee slowly and touch the left knee to the mat. Return to standing position. Touch only the left knee to the mat. Repeat, changing to right knee.

30. Frog Dance

    Take a squat position. Keep the back straight and fold arms across chest at shoulder height. Hop on the left foot and extend right leg straight out to the side. Keep the weight over the supporting left leg, hop again and quickly draw the right leg under the body. At the same time, extend left leg to the side. Continue, alternating the left and right leg extensions.

31. Seal Walk

    Take a prone position. Place hands flat on floor directly under shoulders, fingers to side. Keep ankles extended, weight on top of toes. Progress forward walking with hands, legs and toes dragging.

32. Wheelbarrow races.

F. Rhythm

1. Practice basic locomotor skills varying the rhythm with drum or metronome.

Even	*Uneven*
Walk	Gallop
Run	Skip
Hop	Slide
Jump	Rising/Falling/Opening
Leap	

2. Clapping on floor; if performed in unison, clapping will sound like one clap.
3. Following rhythms with parts of body.
4. Hop scotch (use a long course involving rhythmic changing of the feet)
5. Jump rope; jump on one foot, alternate to the other foot, two feet, etc.
6. Hop in a pattern (i.e., 2 left; 3 right).
7. In circles of three, toss 2 balls or 2 beanbags in unison from player to player. (A rhythm will be developed to accomplish this.)
8. Dramatize rhythms with stories, feelings, ideas.
9. Any and all elementary folk dances.

G. Relaxation

1. Tighten and relax. Concentrate effort on specific areas (i.e., clench fist and let it drop). Child should be lying on back with eyes closed.
2. Lie on stomach, arms out to sides and press against floor.
3. Limp Man Exercise (one person shakes the other's limp limbs).
4. From a standing position with head drooping, breathe in steadily while raising arms horizontally. Then slowly, while breathing out, lift head, lower arms, and let head drop again.
5. Start on the floor, face up, hands on stomach. Each individual should breathe in and out steadily according to her own rhythm. Try to "feel" the abdomen rise and fall when breathing.
6. Start on the back on the floor; slide arms sideways and up in a symmetrical movement with heels of hands meeting overhead. As arms slide up, breathe in, as arms slide down, breathe out.
7. Soothing music.
8. Head circles, followed by head and shoulders circles, followed by head, shoulders, and waist circles. Keep rotations slow, and alternate sides.
9. Stretching exercises.
10. Begin with children lying down with eyes closed. Tell a quiet story about a walk through the forest.
11. Begin with children on backs and relaxed. They slowly raise knees by letting feet slide along the floor toward trunk. Then relax tension in leg muscles and let feet slide back to original position.
12. From position described in 11 above, have children swing legs to right, touch the floor, then to left, touch the floor. Exert as little ef-

fort as possible.

13. Begin with children lying on their backs. Have them lazily roll over to stomachs. Then lazily roll return to starting position.

H. Visual Motor

1. Imitative tasks; follow the leader.
2. Games of "statues." Leader assumes and maintains a pose. Children must imitate poses.
3. Using two inverted paper cups, place a small object (marble, figurine) under one cup. Move cups about. Urge child to keep track of where the object is at all times. As child's skill improves, add more empty cups.
4. Draw and trace patterns. Cut out large geometric shapes. Call out a shape and have child jump to it. Let the child pick a shape and tell you what it is.
5. Dodge ball.
6. Catch, using different sizes and weighted objects.
7. Roll a ball into a box. Bounce a ball into a box.
8. Throw a beanbag into a box.
9. Painting.
10. Etch-A-Sketch.
11. Marsden ball.
12. Frisbee.

I. Trunk Awareness And Differentiation

1. Seat children with backs to wall, arms outstretched at shoulder height. Bend at waist and touch the floor on either side of the body. Don't allow participants to move away from the wall.
2. Pivot upper trunk from side to side, with legs and hips flat on the floor. Hold the child's hips so that only the upper trunk can move. As child pivots to the side have him slide his hands down the side to touch his knee.
3. Have child reach for an object on the floor to the far right or left.
4. Swing upper trunk from side to side.
5. From a sitting position on a mat, lift knees and point them first to the right and then to the left.
6. Bent-knees sit-ups.

J. Internal Directionality

1. Standing in a circle, students follow teacher's instructions. Teacher says, "Raise right foot" (or hip or eyebrow) and all follow. Practice to both left and right. Also have students practice pointing left and right and walking left and right.
2. Pass or bounce a ball to a person on the right or left.
3. Identification. Ask children to identify left and right sides of body. Cross arms over midline and then identify various body parts. (Children sit on floor, knees bent, feet flat on the floor. Teacher calls out directions such as right hand on left knee. After achieving command, students return arms to crossed position.)

K. External Directionality

1. Aiming games (space-structuring).
2. Hiding games (space-structuring).
3. Gymnastics.
4. Aqua tumbling (synchronized swimming).
5. Outdoor adventure activities such as
   a. Orienteering
   b. Ropes course
   c. Map making and reading

CHAPTER XII

COMPUTER GAMES CAN CONTRIBUTE TO ACADEMIC LEARNING

MANY AMERICAN school children spend their spare time with computers programmed for games. Additionally, youngsters are being provided opportunities to learn, think, and compute using computers within their elementary and secondary schools. We will have to find ways for youngsters to move from computer games to more formal computer learning, but given the great amounts of software available, it should not be too difficult to find appropriate programs for each learner.

Many parents are concerned because their youngsters spend too much time in the computer arcades, wasting money and learning nothing. Most parents cannot figure out *what it is* that their children are "hooked on" (Loftus and Loftus, 1983).

POSITIVE REINFORCEMENT

The first thing most youngsters learn about computer games is that when they perform the task requested, they get rewarded; points are tallied up on the scoreboard, a ghost is chewed up and swallowed, an enemy ship disintegrates, etc. For most of us, it is satisfying and habit-forming to get rewarded for efforts and/or skills. Computer games reward according to accomplishment; more effort and/or skill produces greater rewards than less effort and/or skill.

ATTENTION

Players of computer games learn early to heed pertinent information.

If they don't, a "symbolic self" on the screen will be shot down, eaten up, remain numberless or be otherwise destroyed. Attention is the first prerequisite for almost all learning. Without it students cannot focus on what needs to be learned. The capacity to focus with clear figure/ground (Chapter III) is essential to attention. Without it the student cannot distinguish what is important from what is unimportant and she has no way to put value on the information before her. There is no real way of knowing if there is important information to deal with.

Most youngsters learn the nature of computer games by watching someone else play. When the youngster finally has a chance to play, she will learn quickly what she must do to get more positive rewards. She will learn to watch the spooks on the rocks very carefully instead of watching herself. Eventually she will be able to see the importance of their relationship to her position.

DIRECTIONALITY

Once our player learns to focus on the important information, he will learn to react by moving his symbolic self in safe and nondestructive ways. This involves not only being able to tell up from down, right from left and sometimes front from back, but also being able to project these space coordinates within his symbolic self in relation to "the enemy." This is the capacity to apply directionality to the world (Chapter VI), which is essential to reading and writing and arithmetic.

REACTION TIME

Some believe that a person's reaction time is innate and does not change with age, experience, or practice. There is much evidence, however, to indicate that reaction time will decrease when the individual has an expection that something is going to happen in a specific space/time framework (i.e., a monster will appear to my right in one-half second). As the individual experiences the game and the game program, certain repeated patterns will become expected so that reaction time will shorten. Often the individual becomes aware how much her reaction time has improved and begins to help others predict when to expect patterns.

This skill can be transferred to classroom work by teaching students to expect certain words, body language, tones of voice as cues to certain behaviors. (If the teacher gets up from her desk and steps to the right it means recess. The first one in line gets to carry the equipment. When, during a test, the teacher takes a breath in, she is about to ask the next question so I had better pay attention.)

EYE-HAND COORDINATION

Eye-hand coordination involves receiving sensory information and then responding, through movement, with a proper reaction. It is developed through various encounters with the environment so that one learns to interpret incoming information correctly. Eventually the individual will learn to develop a repertoire of responses so that the most appropriate one will be employed for even slight changes in circumstances (Chapter IV).

When playing PacMan,® for instance, most beginners worry only about escaping from the closest monster which causes them to override the joystick and be "flung out of the jaws of one monster and into the jaws of another." After some practice, the beginner will learn to see more than one monster and more than one avenue of escape. In the meantime, the hand controlling the joystick will develop much more finesse in movement appropriate for incoming data so that the player not only escapes a monster but eats an energizer and a monster during the escape. Computers allow endless repetition and drill opportunity.

If we can sort what is to be drilled and what is to be experienced as cognitive strategy development, then the computer can provide multiple individualized activities of the desired kind.

DEVELOPING COGNITIVE STRATEGIES TO BECOME A BETTER GAME PLAYER

As indicated in the eye-hand coordination discussions, even at beginning levels players have strategies and are developing new strategies as fast as possible. The first strategy, "escape from the monster," turns into the second strategy, "escape from two monsters," which turns into the third strategy, "eat an energizer if a monster is approaching." The strategies get increasingly complex as the rewards get better and better.

GUINDON

I'd have much better hand-eye coordination if you'd give me some quarters for the machines.

Figure 8. "Guindon" from the *San Francisco Chronicle*, September 20, 1982, ©by and permission of News America Syndicate.

Further along, our strategist would be developing everything that made her win the greatest number of points in the least amount of time. One element is to learn to delay eating an energizer until a monster comes close, so that the player can eat both energizer and monster in a single short turn. While in the area, she should eat all dots (points) instead of coming back later and taking more time. The player could also learn the shortest routes and thereby reduce time.

One of the main ways of conceptualizing information is to classify it according to kind, type, and category, so that there is a conceptual grouping based upon some quality in common. Does X fit category A or category B? Are those my enemies or my friends? Are those alien ships or sister ships? Classifying of this sort meshes with ways of strategizing in computer games.

Once a person learns to develop cognitive strategies and knows that he is doing so, it is not too difficult for the same individual to develop similar types of strategies for other games or other environmental interactions (even one called school).

We first learn strategies to get what we want or need from our parents, and for some youngsters strategy-making stops there. But it is quite important to develop strategies to deal with brothers and sisters, aunts and uncles, grandparents, the bully in the house around the corner, each different schoolteacher and so on.

LEARNING ABOUT COMPUTERS FOR PERSONAL AND/OR PROFESSIONAL POTENTIAL

Although huge numbers of college students are majoring in computer science, those with lots of hands-on experience are most apt to succeed. Computer games can lead to the abilities to choose positive reinforcement; to develop an attention span; directionality; reaction time; eye-hand coordination; cognitive strategies; and the ability to *learn how to learn* (so that dealing with many kinds of learning skills will be much easier). But in addition, many youngsters with a computer games background are also those who go on to learn all they can about computers at an early age and who ultimately find themselves working or studying within the computer industry. These are people who have developed a thorough understanding of computers as well as a wholesome enjoyment and respect for them.

ACTIVITIES

1. *Rhythm.* With metronome or drum perform each of the movements 8 times while lying on back with eyes closed:
    blink eyes

wink right eye
wink left eye
tongue side to side touching inside of cheek
tongue out and in
scrunch nose
lift right shoulder
lift left shoulder
lift both shoulders
breathe in and out
abdomen in and out
lift right hip
lift left hip
lift right knee
lift left knee
lift both knees
kick right foot
kick left foot
kick both feet
lift right elbow
lift left elbow
lift both elbows
shake right hand
shake left hand
shake both hands

Increase complexity. Lying on back, bend and straighten right leg, then bend and straighten right leg while raising and lowering right arm. Do same with left leg and left arm. Alternate sides. Bend and straighten right leg while raising and lowering left arm. Same with left leg and right arm. Alternate. Increase speed. Finally, do the entire sequence standing (see Barsch, 1968).

CHAPTER XIII

WHERE TO GO FROM HERE

WHAT DOES IT ALL MEAN?

WE HAVE KNOWN for several years that the only way to get information about the external world is through our sensory systems. And we have known for several years that the only way to express ourselves to others is through our motoric systems (which allow us to speak, write, kiss, hit, etc.). So it comes as no surprise that the ultimate union of these systems is the basis for learning.

We have known for several years that the mind and body are ONE, a unity, but we have continued to *speak* as though they were separate. We have continued to use *words* as our main teaching method instead of *experiences*.

If we have youngsters who are not learning effectively in the public schools, we must find ways to adjust elements of the systems and/or the interrelationships between these elements for each of those individuals. Teachers must create new programs that utilize these components because they will result in effective teaching methods for many students.

When, with students who can't read, we make them continue to "read" over and over material that is beyond them, we waste their time and self-respect. We need ways to teach a student how to identify various symbols like

while he is standing on his head, or as he moves past (while holding onto others in a circle).

Teachers everywhere must learn more and more about computers, computer games, and computer graphics so they can develop new ways to encourage figure/ground awareness in some students, directionality in others, and balance for some.

We need to consider some of the newer programs.

Kamii and DeVries (1980), operating from the perspective of Piaget, demonstrate what children can learn from their newly-created group games and how they maximize learning. Kamii and DeVries are careful to spell out the cognitive value of the various games they use. "All aiming games are good for the structuring of space because children think about spatial relationships when they try to direct an object toward a specific spot . . . All races provide opportunities for making comparisons. Some offer the possibility of ordering people's arrival in time." They continue the analysis through chasing games, guessing games, games involving verbal commands, card games, board games. Their book is filled with excellent descriptions and analyses of games in all of these categories.

Laura Meyers and Teresa Rosegrant (Trachtman, 1983) are working with exceptional children who have little, if any, language of their own. The most remarkable thing about their program is that they have used computers with these youngsters in such a way that they begin to speak. Meyers and Rosegrant's tale is a remarkable one, involving much success with computers and children.

Terry Orlick (1978) has made strides with an approach to learning that consists of games but not the usual kinds of games. He calls them "cooperative games." The following are brief descriptions of a very few of his games. Students learn some things much more easily when competition is not involved.

Toesies

Partners lie stretched out on the floor, feet to feet (or big toe to big toe) and attempt to roll across the floor, keeping their toes touching throughout.

Beach Ball Balance

One beach ball or balloon is shared by two who try to hold the ball between them without hands. See how many different ways (head to head, side to side, etc.) can be utilized. Then move around room or obstacle course using beach balls in many different points of contact.

Frozen Beanbag

All move around the room at own pace while balancing a beanbag on their heads (no hands). Leader can change action or pace by saying: skip, hop, go backward, go slower, faster, etc. If the bag falls off the head, that person is frozen. Another person must pick up beanbag and place it on that person's head to free him, without losing one's own bag. The object is to help each other. At the end ask how many people were helped.

Partner Pull-Up

Partners sit down facing each other, with soles of feet on floor, toes touching. They reach forward and grasp hands. By pulling, both come up to standing. Then sit the same way.

Logroll

Several people lie down on mat, side by side. A rider lies on his stomach perpendicular to the logs. All logs then begin rolling in the same direction, giving the rider a soft or bumpy ride. The rider becomes a log and one log becomes the rider.

Collective Blanketball

Two teams of 4-8 each spread around 2 sturdy blankets and grasp edges while a ball is placed in the middle of one blanket. Teams toss one ball back and forth, like volleyball. To keep score, count one point for each time the ball is tossed over the net and caught.

ACTIVITIES

1. Sit down at your desk with pen in hand and think about some of the programs discussed in this chapter. Now think of an elementary school game that you have played which was truly valueless or worse, for you. Think long enough to determine how you would make that game of value to students presently in elementary school.
2. Can you think of moe games to change? And ways to change them?

3. Perhaps you can send these new games to Kamii and DeVries or to Orlick for their new books. I'm sure they will be grateful and glad to hear from you.

BIBLIOGRAPHY

Abt, Clark C.: *Serious Games.* New York, The Viking Press, 1970.

Agnew, Neil McK., and Pyke, Sandra W.: *The Science Game: An Introduction to Research in the Behavioral Sciences.* Englewood Cliffs, Prentice-Hall, 1978.

American Association for Health, Physical Education, and Recreation: *Annotated Bibliography on Perceptual-Motor Development.* Washington, D.C., AAHPER, 1973.

Arena, John: *Teaching Through Sensory-Motor Experiences.* San Rafael, Academic Therapy Pub., 1969.

Arnheim, Daniel D., and Pestolesi, Robert A.: *Elementary Physical Education: A Developmental Approach, 2nd ed.* St. Louis, C.V. Mosby Co., 1978.

Arnheim, Daniel D., Auxter, David, and Crowe, Walter C.: *Adapted Physical Education and Recreation.* St. Louis, C.V. Mosby, 1977.

Ayres, A. Jean: *Perceptual-Motor Dysfunction in Children.* Monograph from the Greater Cincinnati District Ohio Occupational Therapy Association Conference, 1964.

Ayres, A.: *Sensory Integration and Learning Disorders.* Los Angeles, Western Psychological Services, 1973.

Ayres, A.: *Southern California Perceptual-Motor Tests Manual.* Los Angeles, Western Psychological Services, 1973.

Bartenieff, Irmgard, and Lewis, Dori: *Body Movement: Coping With the Environment.* New York, Gordon and Breach Sciences Pub., Inc., 1980.

Bateson, Gregory: *Mind and Nature: A Necessary Unity.* New York, E.P. Dutton, 1979.

Ball, Thomas S.: *Itard, Seguin, and Kephart: Sensory Education — A Learning Interpretation.* Columbus, Chas. E. Merrill, 1971.

Ball, Thomas S., and Edgar, Clara Lee: The effectiveness of sensorimotor training in promoting generalized body image development. *The Journal of Special Education,* vol. 1, no. 4, Summer, 1967.

Barnes, Joan, and Astor, Susan D. with Tosi, Umberto: *GYMBOREE: Giving Your Child Physical, Mental and Social Confidence Through Play.* Garden City, Dolphin Books, 1981.

Barnett, Lincoln: *The Universe and Dr. Einstein.* New York, Mentor, 1952.

Barsch, Ray H.: *Achieving Perceptual-Motor Efficiency.* Seattle, Special Child Publications, 1968.

Barsch, Ray H.: *Enriching Perception and Cognition.* Seattle, Special Child Publication, 1969.

Bekesy, von, Georg: *Sensory Inhibition*. Princeton, Princeton University Press, 1962.

Belluzzi, James D.: personal communication. Professor of Physiological Psychology, California State University, Chico, 1972.

Bobath, Berta: *Abnormal Postural Reflex Activity Caused by Brain Lesions*. London, William Heinemann Medical Books, Ltd., 1971.

Bobath, Berta, and Bobath, Karel: *Motor Development In The Different Types of Cerebral Palsy*. London, William Heinemann Medical Books, Ltd., 1975.

Braun, Samuel J., and Edwards, Esther P.: *History and Theory of Early Childhood Education*. Worthington, Chas. A. Jones, 1972.

Broer, Marion: *Efficiency of Human Movement*. Philadelphia, W.B. Saunders, 1973.

Capon, Jack: *Perceptual Motor Development: Basic Movement Activities*. El Segundo, Prismatica International, 1974.

Chaney, Clara M., and Kephart, Newell C.: *Motoric Aids to Perceptual Training*. Columbus, Chas. E. Merrill, 1974.

Chaney, Clara M., and Miles, Nancy R.: *Remediating Learning Problems: A Developmental Curriculum*. Columbus, Chas. E. Merrill, 1974.

Cochran, Norman A., Wilkinson, Lloyd C., and Furlow, John J.: *Learning on the Move*. Dubuque, Kendall/Hunt, 1981.

Combs, Arthur W., Richard, Anne Cohen, and Richards, Fred: *Perceptual Psychology*. New York, Harper & Row, 1976.

Cratty, Bryant: *Movement Behavior and Motor Learning*. Philadelphia, Lea and Febiger, 1973.

Cratty, Bryant: *Intelligence in Action: Physical Activities for Enhancing Intellectual Abilities*. Englewood Cliffs, Prentice-Hall, 1973.

Cratty, Bryant J.: *Psy-Motor Behavior In Education and Sport*. Springfield, Charles C Thomas, 1974.

Curtis, Sandra: *The Joy of Movement*. New York, Teachers College Press, 1982.

Darst, Paul W., and Armstrong, George P.: *Outdoor Adventure Activities for School and Recreation Programs*. Minneapolis, Burgess, 1980.

Delacato, Carl: *The Diagnosis and Treatment of Speech and Reading Problems*. Springfield, Charles C Thomas, 1964.

Delacato, Carl: *Neurological Organization and Reading*. Springfield, Charles C Thomas, 1967.

Delgado, Jose M.R.: *Physical Control of the Mind*. New York, Harper Colophon, 1969.

Delgado, Jose M.R.: Brain manipulation: psycho-civilized direction of behavior. *The Humanist,* March/April, 1972.

Dickinson, John: *Proprioceptive Control of Human Movement*. London, Lepus, 1974.

Doman, Glenn: *Teach Your Body Math*. New York, Simon and Schuster, 1979.

Drawatzky, John: *Motor Learning: Principles and Practices*. Minneapolis, Burgess, 1981.

Edelman, Gerald, and Mountcastle, Vernon B.: *The Mindful Brain*. MIT Press, 1982.

Edgar, Clara Lee: Perceptual-motor training as an aid to development of reading skills. In Douglass, Malcom P.: *Reading In Education, A Broader View*. Columbus, Chas. E. Merrill, 1967.

Edgar, Clara Lee: *The Santa Cruz Special Education Information Management System* (SEIMS). Office of Santa Cruz County Superintendent of Schools, Santa Cruz, 1979.

Edgar, Clara Lee, Ball, Thomas S., McIntyre, Robert B., and Shotwell, Anna M.: Effects of sensory-motor training of adoptive behavior. *American Journal of Mental Deficiency,* vol. 73, no. 5, March, 1969.

Edgar, Clara Lee, Kohler, Hugh F., and Hardman, Scott: A new method for toilet training developmentally disabled children. *Perceptual and Motor Skills,* vol. 41, pp. 63-69, 1975.

Edie, James M. (Ed.): *The Primacy of Perception, Maurice Merleau-Ponty.* Chicago, Northwestern University Press, 1964.

Fait, Hollis F.: *Physical Education for the Elementary School Child.* Philadelphia, W.B. Saunders, 1976.

Ferguson, Sandi: Conference at California State University Chico, 1975.

Fisher, Seymour: *Body Consciousness.* Englewood Cliffs, Prentice-Hall, 1973.

Fisher, Seymour, and Cleveland, Sidney: *Body Image.* Princeton, D. Van Nostrand, 1958.

Flavell, John H.: *The Developmental Psychology of Jean Piaget.* New York, D. Van Nostrand, 1963.

Flinchum, Betty M.: *Motor Development in Early Childhood.* St. Louis, C.V. Mosby, 1975.

Fowler, W., and Leithwood, K.A.: Cognition and movement: theoretical, pedagogical, and measurement considerations, *Perceptual and Motor Skills,* vol. 32, pp. 523-532, 1971.

Frostig, Marianne: *Administration and Scoring Manual for the Marianne Frostig Developmental Test of Visual Perception.* Palo Alto, Consulting Psychologist Press, 1966.

Frostig, Marianne, and Maslow, Phyllis: *Frostig MGL: Move, Grow, Learn.* Chicago, Follett, 1969.

Frostig, Marianne, and Maslow, Phyllis: *Learning Problems in the Classroom.* New York, Grune and Stratton, 1973.

Furth, Hans G.: *Piaget and Knowledge.* Englewood Cliffs, Prentice-Hall, 1969.

Furth, Hans, and Wachs, Harry: *Thinking Goes to School: Piaget's Theory in Practice.* New York, Oxford University Press, 1974.

Gallahue, David L.: *Motor Development and Movement Experiences for Young Children.* New York, John Wiley and Sons, 1976.

Gazzaniga, Michale: *The Bisected Brain.* New York, Appleton-Century-Crofts, 1970.

Gesell, A.: *The First Five Years of Life.* New York, Harper and Brothers, 1940.

Gesell, Arnold: *How a Baby Grows.* New York, Harper & Row, 1945.

Getman, G.N.: *How to Develop Your Child's Intelligence.* Luverne, Announcer Press, 1965.

Getman, Gerald N.: *Pathway.* Boston, Program I Teaching Resources Corporation, 1970.

Gibson, Eleanor J.: *Principles of Perceptual Learning and Development.* New York, Meredith, 1969.

Gibson, Eleanor, and Levin, Harry: *The Psychology of Reading.* Cambridge, MIT Press, 1975.

Gibson, James J: *The Ecological Approach to Visual Perception.* Boston, Houghton Mifflin, 1979.

Ginsburg, Herbert, and Opper, Sylvia: *Piaget's Theory of Intellectual Development: An In-*

troduction. Englewood Cliffs, Prentice-Hall, 1969.

Gitter, Lena L.: *The Montessori Way.* Seattle, Special Child Publications, 1970.

Godfrey, Barbara B., and Kephart, Newell C: *Movement Patterns and Motor Education.* New York, Appleton-Century-Crofts, 1969.

Gunderson, Ed J.: A note on the "so-called" mind-body problem. *ETC*, vol. XXXII, no. 3, pp. 317-320:1971.

Harrow, Anita J.: *A Taxonomy of the Psychomotor Domain.* New York, David McKay, 1972.

Hart, Leslie: *How the Brain Works.* New York, Basic Books, 1975.

Hart, Leslie A.: Brain-compatible teaching. *Today's Education.* pp. 42-45, Nov.-Dec. 1978.

Hebb, D.O.: *The Organization of Behavior: A Neuropsychological Theory.* New York, Science Editions, 1961.

Hebb, D.O.: *Textbook of Psychology.* Philadelphia, W.B. Saunders, 1972.

Held, Richard: Plasticity in sensory-motor systems. In *Perception Mechanism and Models: Readings from Scientific American,* Ch. 38. San Francisco, W.H. Freeman, 1972.

Hoffman, Donald D.: The interpretation of visual illusions. *Scientific American,* December 1983, vol. 249, no. 6, pp. 137-146.

Hoffman, Hubert A., Young, Jane, and Klesius, Stephen E.: *Meaningful Movement for Children.* Boston, Allyn & Bacon, 1981.

Humphrey, James H., and Humphrey, Joy N.: *Help Your Child Learn the 3 R's Through Active Play.* Springfield, Charles C Thomas, 1980.

Hunt, Valerie: Personal communication. UCLA, Los Angeles, 1958.

Inhelder, Barbel, and Piaget, Jean: *The Growth of Logical Thinking.* New York, Basic Books, 1958.

Isaacs, Nathan: *A Brief Introduction to Piaget.* New York, Schocken, 1974.

Jacobson, Edmund: *Progressive Relaxation.* Chicago, University of Chicago Press, 1938.

Jones, Harold E.: *Motor Performance and Growth.* Berkeley, University of California, 1949.

Jones, Margaret, Hunt, Valerie, and Barrett, Mary: Movement and behavior patterns of young cerebral palsied children in a small confined space. *Journal of Neurology and Child Behavior,* London, March 1967.

Kamii, Constance, and DeVries, Rheta: *Physical Knowledge in Preschool Education: Implications of Piaget's Theory.* Englewood Cliffs, Prentice-Hall, 1978.

Kamii, Constance, and DeVries, Rheta: *Group Games in Early Education.* Washington, DC, The National Association for the Education of Young Children, 1980.

Kelley, Earl: *Education for What is Real.* New York, Harper & Brothers, 1947.

Kephart, Newell C.: *Learning Disability: An Educational Adventure.* West Lafayette, Kappa Delta Pi Press, 1968.

Kephart, Newell: *The Slow Learner in the Classroom.* Columbus, Chas. E. Merrill, 1971.

Kidd, Olive H., and Rivoire, Jeanne L. (Eds.): *Perceputal Development in Children.* New York, International Universities Press, 1971.

Kirk, Samuel A., and Lord, Francis E.: *Exceptional Children: Educational Resources and Perspectives.* Boston, Houghton Mifflin, 1974.

Lawrence, Connie C., and Hackett, Layne C.: *Water Learning: A New Adventure.* Palo Alto, Peek Publications, 1975.

Leithwood, Kenneth A.: Motor, cognitive and affective relationships among advantaged preschool children. *The Research Quarterly,* vol. 42, no. 1, pp. 47-53, 1971.

Lerch, Harold A., Becker, John E., Ward, Bonnie M., and Nelson, Judith A.: *Perceptual-Motor Learning: Theory and Practice.* Palo Alto, Peek Publications, 1974.

Levitt, Robert A.: *Psychopharmacology: A Biological Approach.* New York, John Wiley, 1975.

Liess, Andreas: *Carl Orff.* London, Calder and Boyars, 1966.

Llinas, Rodolfo R.: The cortex of the cerebellum. *Scientific American,* January, 1972.

Loftus, Geoffrey R., and Loftus, Elizabeth F.: *Mind at Play.* New York, Basic Books, 1983.

Lovell, K.: *The Growth of Basic Mathematical and Scientific Concepts in Children.* London, University of London, 1961.

Luria, A.R.: *Human Brain and Psychological Processes.* New York, Harper and Row, 1966.

Luria, A.R.: *The Working Brain.* New York, Basic Books, 1973.

Magill, Richard: *Motor Learning: Concepts and Applications.* Dubuque, Wm. C. Brown, 1980.

Maloney, Michael P., Ball, Thomas S., and Edgar, Clara Lee: Analysis of the generalizability of sensory-motor training. *American Journal of Mental Deficiency,* vol. 74, no. 4, January, pp. 458-468, 1970.

Manual for Lincoln-Oseretsky Motor Development Scale, #37018, General Monographs, 1955:51, pp. 183-252, C.H. Stoelting Co., Chicago, 1954.

Marr, David: *Vision.* W.H. Freeman & Company, San Francisco, 1982.

Marteniuk, Ronald G.: *Information Processing in Motor Skills.* New York, Holt Rinehart and Winston, 1976.

Meyers, Russell: The proprioceptive matrix of abstractions called mass, energy, space and time. *ETC.,* pp. 389-495, December, 1976.

Miles, Nancy R.: *Swimming Techniques for Children with Learning Disabilities.* Chicago, Developmental Learning Materials, 1970.

Miller, George A., and Lennesberg, Elizabeth, (Eds.): *Psychology and Biology of Language and Thought.* Orlando, Academic Press, 1978.

Milner, Peter: *Physiological Psychology.* New York, Rinehart and Winston, 1970.

Montessori, Maria: *The Montessori Methods.* Cambridge, Robert Bentley, 1967.

Murray, Ruth Lovell: *Dance in Elementary Education.* New York, Harper and Row, 1975.

Neisser, Ulric: *Cognition and Reality: Principles and Implications of Cognitive Psychology.* San Francisco, W.H. Freeman, 1976.

Orlick, Terry: *The Cooperative Sports and Games Book.* New York, Pantheon, 1978.

Pearce, Joseph C.: *Magical Child.* New York, E.P. Dutton, 1977.

Petitclerc, Grace: *Learning With the Challenging Child.* San Rafael, Academic Therapy Publications, 1971.

Phillips, John L.: *The Origins of Intellect: Piaget's Theory.* San Francisco, W.H. Freeman, 1975.

Piaget, Jean: *The Origins of Intelligence in Children.* New York, International Universities

Press, 1952.

————: *The Construction of Reality in the Child.* New York, Ballantine, 1954.

————: *Play, Dreams and Imitation in Childhood.* New York, W.W. Morton, 1962.

————: *Judgement and Reasoning in the Child.* Paterson, Littlefield, Adams & Co., 1964.

————: *The Child's Conception of the World.* Totowa, Littlefield, Adams & Co., 1965.

————: *Structuralism.* New York, Harper Colophon, 1970a.

————: *The Child's Conception of Movement and Speed.* New York, Ballantine, 1970b.

————: *Genetic Epistemology.* New York, W.W. Morton, 1970c.

————: *The Child's Conception of Physical Reality.* Totowa, Littlefield, Adams & Co., 1972.

————: *The Child and Reality.* New York, Penguin, 1976.

————, and Inhelder, Barbel: *The Psychology of the Child.* New York, Basic Books, 1969.

Piers, Maria W., and Landau, Genevieve M.: *The Gift of Play.* New York, Walker & Co., 1980.

Pietsch, Paul: *Shuffle-Brain.* Boston, Houghton-Mifflin, 1981.

Pribram, Karl H.: *Languages of the Brain.* Englewood Cliffs, Prentice-Hall, 1971.

Radler, D.H., and Kephart, Newell C.: *Success Through Play.* New York, Harper and Row, 1969.

Raker, Betty Lou: *A Study of Life Style in Cognition and Movement.* Ann Arbor, University Microfilms, 1969.

Reynolds, Allan G., and Flagg, Paul W.: *Cognitive Psychology.* Cambridge, Winthrop, 1977.

Richmond, P.G.: *An Introduction to Piaget.* New York, Basic Books, 1970.

Roach, Eugene G., and Kephart, Newell C.: *The Purdue Perceptual-Motor Survey.* Columbus, Chas. E. Merrill, 1966.

Rousseau, Jean Jacques: *Emile.* New York, Dutton, 1969.

Sage, George H.: *Introduction to Motor Behavior: A Neuropsychological Approach.* Reading, Addison-Wesley, 1971.

Schilder, Paul: *The Image and Appearance of the Human Body.* New York, International Universities Press, 1950.

Schneider, Allen M., and Tarshis, Barry: *An Introduction to Physiological Psychology.* New York, Random House, 1975.

Scientific American: *Physiological Psychology.* San Francisco, W.H. Freeman, 1972.

Scientific American: *Perception: Mechanisms and Models.* San Francisco, W.H. Freeman, 1972.

Shears, Loyda, and Bower, Eli M.: *Games in Education and Development.* Springfield, Charles C Thomas, 1974.

Simmons, Anne, Porter, Marcella, and Norman, Irene: *Child's Play.* Springfield, Charles C Thomas, 1982.

Singer, Robert N.: *Motor Learning and Human Performance.* New York, MacMillan, 1980.

Skinner, Louise: *Motor Development in The Preschool Years.* Springfield, Charles C Thomas, 1979.

Sloan, William: The Lincoln-Oseretsky motor development scale. *Genetic Psychology*

Monographs, vol. 51, pp. 183-252, 1955.

Smith, Paul: *Perceptual Motor Test.* Palo Alto, Peek Publications, 1973.

Smith, Karl V., and Smith William M.: *Perception and Motion.* Philadelphia, W.B. Saunders, 1962.

Sperry, R.W.: The great cerebal commission. *Scientific American,* vol. 210(1), pp. 42-52, 1964.

Stelmach, George E. (Ed.): *Motor Control Issues and Trends.* Orlando, Academic Press, 1976.

Tart, Charles T.: Physiological correlates of psi cognition. *International Journal of Parapsychology,* vol. 5, pp. 375-386, 1963.

Tart, Charles T.: *States of Consciousness.* New York, E.P. Dutton, 1975.

Trachtman, Paul: Putting computers into the hands of children without language. *Smithsonian,* February 1984, vol. 14, no. 11, pp. 42-51.

Uttal, William R.: *The Psychobiology of Sensory Coding.* New York, Harper and Row, 1973.

Wadsworth, Barry J.: *Piaget's Theory of Cognitive Development.* New York, Longman, 1971.

Wadsworth, Barry, J.: *Piaget for the Classroom Teacher.* New York, Longman, 1978.

Warner, Lynn D.: *Dynamic Balance and Its Relationship to Reading Achievement.* Unpublished Masters Thesis, Humboldt State University, 1970.

Watts, Alan: *The Book: On the Taboo Against Knowing Who You Are.* New York, Collier Books, 1966.

Webber, Irma E.: *It Looks Like This.* San Francisco, International Society for General Semantics, 1976.

Werner, Peter H., and Burton, Elsie C.: *Learning Through Movement.* St. Louis, C.V. Mosby, 1979.

Whiting, H.T.A.: *Acquiring Ball Skill: A Psychological Interpretation.* Philadelphia, Lea and Febiger, 1969.

Williams, Harriet G.: *Perceptual and Motor Development.* Englewood Cliffs, Prentice-Hall, 1983.

Winnick, Joseph P., and French, Ronald W. (Eds.): *Piaget for Regular and Special Physical Educators and Recreators.* Brockport, State University College, 1975.

Witkin, H.A., Lewis, H.B., Hertzman, M., Machover, K., Meissner, P.B., and Wapner, S.: *Personality Thorugh Perception.* New York, Harper & Brothers, 1954.

Wolff, Sydney, and Wolff, Caryl: *Games Without Words.* Springfield, Charles C Thomas, 1974.

Yawkey, Thomas Daniels (Ed.): *The Self-Concept of The Young Child.* Salt Lake City, Brigham Young University Press, 1980.

Zion, Leela C.: *Body Concept As It Relates to Self Concept.* Ann Arbor, University Microfilms, 1963.

INDEX

143